GUIDE TO FLOOR AND CARPETING INSTALLATION AND REPAIR

McGraw-Hill Book Company

New York   St. Louis   San Francisco   Auckland   Bogotá   Guatemala   Hamburg
Johannesburg   Lisbon   London   Madrid   Mexico   Montreal   New Delhi
Panama   Paris   San Juan   São Paulo   Singapore   Sydney   Tokyo   Toronto

McGraw-Hill Paperbacks Home Improvement Series

Guide to Plumbing

Guide to Electrical Installation and Repair

Guide to Roof and Gutter Installation and Repair

Guide to Wallpaper and Paint

Guide to Paneling and Wallboard

Guide to Landscape and Lawn Care

Guide to Brick, Concrete, and Stonework

Guide to Carpentry

Guide to Furniture Refinishing and Antiquing

Guide to Bathroom and Kitchen Remodeling

Guide to Reupholstering

Guide to Vegetable Gardening and Preserving

Guide to Bicycle Repair and Maintenance

Guide to Floor and Carpeting Installation and Repair

1 2 3 4 5 6 7 8 9 0 SMSM 8 6 5 4 3 2 1

Library of Congress Cataloging in Publication Data

Main entry under title:

Guide to floor and carpeting installation and repair.

(McGraw-Hill paperbacks home improvement series)
Originally published in 1975 by the Automotive-Hardware
Trades Division of Minnesota Mining and Manufacturing Co.,
under title: The home pro floor and carpeting installation and repair
guide.
1. Floors — Amateurs' manuals. 2. Carpets — Amateurs'
manuals. I. Minnesota Mining and Manufacturing Company.
Automotive-Hardware Trades Division. Home pro floor and
carpeting installation and repair guide.
TH2521.G84 698'.9 80-17741
ISBN 0-07-045970-3 (pbk.)

Front cover photo courtesy of Masonite Corporation.

Back cover photo, top, courtesy of Congoleum Corporation:
Ultraflor Majestic "Cameo" flooring.

Back cover photo, center, courtesy of Bigelow-Sanford, Inc.
A Sperry and Hutchinson Company.

Back cover photo, bottom, courtesy of American Olean Tile Company.

Contents

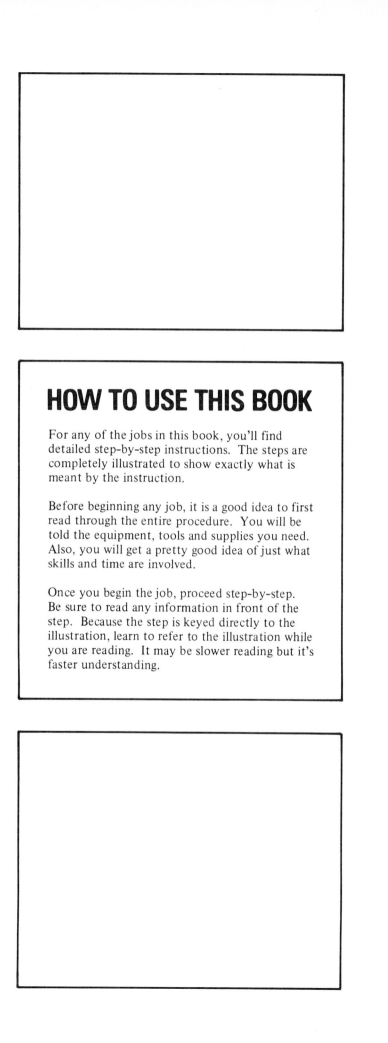

HOW TO USE THIS BOOK

For any of the jobs in this book, you'll find detailed step-by-step instructions. The steps are completely illustrated to show exactly what is meant by the instruction.

Before beginning any job, it is a good idea to first read through the entire procedure. You will be told the equipment, tools and supplies you need. Also, you will get a pretty good idea of just what skills and time are involved.

Once you begin the job, proceed step-by-step. Be sure to read any information in front of the step. Because the step is keyed directly to the illustration, learn to refer to the illustration while you are reading. It may be slower reading but it's faster understanding.

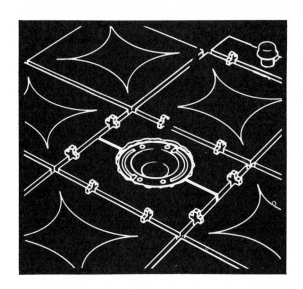

CERAMIC AND MOSAIC FLOORS

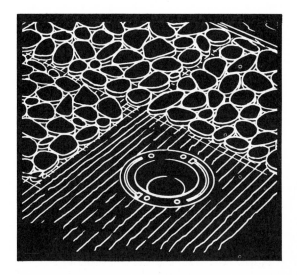

1

Ceramic tiles and mosaic tile sheets are both made from very hard glazed tiles which are durable and easily cleaned. They are also non-fading in color and unaffected by moisture or heat.

Because of these characteristics, ceramic tiles and mosaic sheets are often found in bathrooms, kitchens and entryways. However, tiles or sheets may be used in most areas of the home, both interior and exterior. Their durable characteristics and decorative appearance make them one of the best floor coverings available.

Tiles and sheets are both applied to existing floors with adhesives. After the adhesive has dried, grout is used to fill all gaps and spaces between the tiles.

Because of the very hard, non-flexible surface formed by tiles, it is extremely important that the supporting floor be extremely rigid and even.

Tiles and sheets may be applied to the following floor surfaces;

- Concrete
- Vinyl
- Wood

However, do not install tile over a hardwood floor. Hardwood flooring may warp, causing tiles to crack.

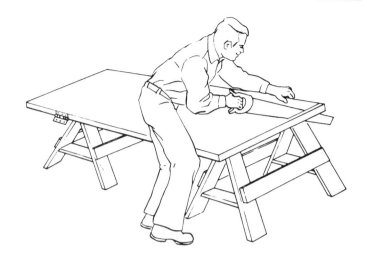

Before beginning to install a sheet or tile floor be sure to consider drying time for adhesive and grout. Because of the amount of time needed for them to dry, the floor being covered cannot be used for a minimum of 48 hours.

Whenever ceramic tiles or mosaic sheets are installed on an existing floor, the height of the floor is raised by approximately 1/2-inch. Therefore, if a door opens across this floor, the door may have to be shortened by 1/2-inch to clear the tile.

▶ Ceramic Tiles

Ceramic tiles are available in a variety of shapes and sizes. The shape and size most commonly used by non-professionals is the 6 x 6 inch square or the 8 x 8 inch square.

Ceramic tiles are available in almost countless patterns, designs, and colors.

Tiles may have self-contained patterns which do not require matching to other tiles. In other cases, a combination of tiles may be needed to form a pattern. Each individual tile is used in combination with other tiles to form a pattern.

Floor patterns can often be varied by combining different sizes, shapes, and colors of tiles. When mixing shapes, colors, and sizes be sure that all tiles are the same thickness.

Tile dealers and some large department stores have a large selection of tiles. These stores may also have qualified people who can help you select tiles.

Be sure you tell the dealer you are installing floor tiles. Wall tiles cannot ordinarily be installed on a floor.

▶ Mosaic Tile Sheets

Mosaic tile sheets consist of many small ceramic tiles attached to a paper backing or web backing. They are available in sheets ranging in size from 6 x 12 inches to 12 x 24 inches.

Until recently some of these sheets had a protective front paper to protect the tiles during installation. This type of sheet is seldom found anymore, but if you should purchase sheets with a front protective paper, they are installed the same as other sheets. However, after the sheets are laid, the paper must be removed before grout is applied.

Mosaic tile sheets are available in many varieties of patterns and colors. The individual tiles may be arranged in a geometric pattern with all tiles the same size and the same distance apart.

They are also available with random patterns in which the individual tiles vary in size and in distance between the tiles.

Tile dealers and some large department stores have a large selection of mosaic sheets. These stores may also have qualified people who can help you select sheets.

▶ Adhesives

There are two types of adhesives that can be used with ceramic tiles or mosaic sheets:

- Mastic Adhesives
- Thin Set Mortar

Mastic adhesive can be used to install tiles or sheets to vinyl, wood, or concrete floors.

Thin set mortar is used on concrete floors only.

Before selecting an adhesive, consult with a tile dealer. He will advise you on the adhesive to use for your particular floor.

▶ Grout

Spaces between tiles are filled with a thin mortar called grout.

Originally all grout was white. However, grout is now available in a variety of colors. Colored grout is used for the decorative effect and to make any soiling less apparent.

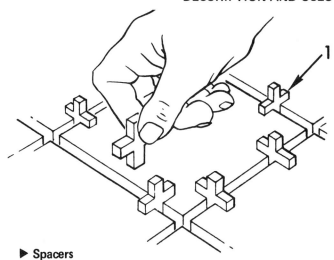

▶ Spacers

Spacers [1] are used for installing ceramic tiles only. They are small pieces made to fit between the tiles to insure that all tiles are installed the same distance apart.

Spacers come in sizes ranging from 1/8 inch to 1/4 inch. Generally the larger the tile the larger the spacer used. However, the size of the space between tiles is something you must determine.

PLANNING AND ESTIMATING

Install a ceramic tile or mosaic sheet floor in the following sequence:

- Determine the pattern, color, size and shape of the tiles or sheets.

- Remove shoe moldings or baseboards.

- Estimate the amount of materials needed, Page 4. Purchase or rent any needed tools and supplies.

- Check the floor surface. Page 4.

- Square off the floor. Page 5.

- Install tiles, Page 7 or sheets, Page 10.

- Apply grout. Page 15.

- Install shoe molding or baseboards. Page 16.

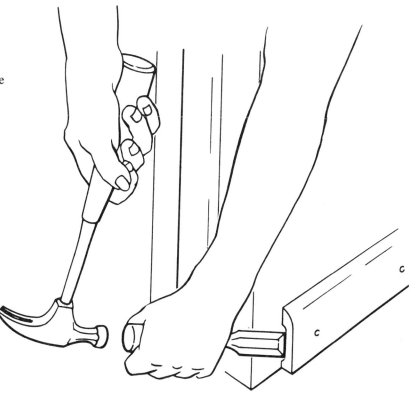

PLANNING AND ESTIMATING

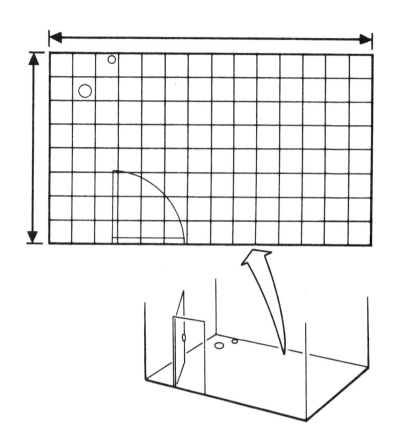

To estimate the amount of materials needed you should make a detailed sketch of the floor to be covered. Graph paper is very handy for making this sketch.

Measure and record all dimensions on the sketch.

Take the sketch to dealer to help determine the following:

● Number of tiles or sheets needed.

● Amount of adhesive needed.

● Amount of grout needed.

If you are installing tiles, the dealer will also tell you the number of spacers needed.

CHECKING FLOOR SURFACES

Ceramic tile floors and mosaic tile floors may be installed on the following surfaces:

● Wood

● Concrete

● Resilient

Because a ceramic floor is very rigid, the surface must be rigid. Any movement in the subsurface will cause the grout to crack and chip and may even cause the tiles to break.

Also, the subsurface must be even. Any high or low spots will cause the grout to crack and possibly cause the tiles to break.

Before beginning to install a tile floor, carefully check the floor and make any necessary repairs.

▶ Checking a Wood Floor

A wood floor must be firm, even, and clean before ceramic tiles or mosaic sheets can be installed.

1. Check to see that floor is firm and does not move or flex.

If floor is not firm it must be made firm.

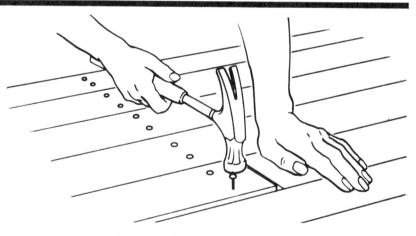

2. Check the floor for the following problems:

● Protruding nails

● Loose boards

● High or low spots

● Cracks or gaps

If any problems are found, they must be repaired.

A commercial wax remover should be used to remove all old wax from the floor.

3. Remove all old wax from floor.

4

▶ **Checking a Concrete Floor**

A concrete floor must be level, clean and sealed before ceramic tiles or mosaic sheets can be installed.

1. Check the floor for the following problems:
    - High or low spots
    - Cracks or gaps
    - Moisture

If any problems are found, they must be repaired.

2. Clean floor surface to remove all oil, dirt, or grease.

Floor must be sealed to provide a bonding surface for the adhesive. Ask a paint dealer what sealer should be used.

3. Seal floor.

▶ **Checking a Resilient Floor**

A resilient floor must be even and clean before ceramic tiles or mosaic sheets can be installed.

1. Check the floor for the following problems:
    - Loose tiles or pieces
    - Cracks or holes

If any problems are found they must be repaired.

A commercial wax remover, should be used to remove all old wax from the floor.

2. Remove all old wax from floor.

━━━ **SQUARING OFF A FLOOR** ━━━━━━━━━━━━━━━━━━━━━━━━

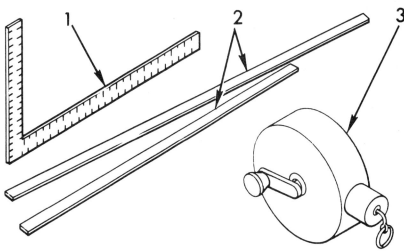

The lines of grout between the tiles in a ceramic tile floor form a pattern of straight lines. Any slanting of these lines would be immediately apparent. Because of this, it is important to lay out a tile floor so that it looks straight.

The walls of a room may not be exactly straight or square with regard to one another. Therefore, a wall should not be used as a guide for laying out the floor. Instead, a doorway should be used as a reference point for laying out the floor. The tile floor should look straight to a person entering the room. If the room has more than one doorway, the most used doorway should be selected as the reference point.

The procedures in this section show how to square off a floor, using a doorway as a reference point. Although these procedures are particularly recommended for laying out a ceramic tile floor, they may also be used for laying out mosaic sheets.

The following tools and supplies are required:

Carpenter's square [1]
Two straight, thin boards [2]. One board must be as long as the width of the room. The other board must be as long as the length of the room. Be sure that these boards are straight because they will be used as guides for installing the tile.
Chalk line [3]

1. Using straightedge, make a line [1] across doorway.

2. Mark center of line [1].

3. Align carpenter's square with center of line [1] to form a 90 degree angle.

4. Align chalk line with edge of carpenter's square. Fasten end of chalk line to floor.

5. Keeping chalk line aligned with carpenter's square, pull other end of chalk line to wall [3].

6. While holding chalk line tight, pull chalk line straight up from floor and release it. Chalk line will mark a straight line [2] from doorway to wall [3].

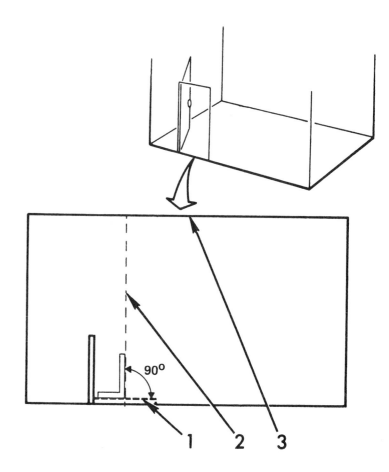

In Steps 7 through 14, the object is to determine the locations of boards used as guides for laying tile.

7. Starting at doorway, determine number of whole tiles which will fit between doorway and wall [1]. Be sure to allow for width of gap between each tile. Width of gap is determined by measuring thickness of spacers. See Page 3 for description of spacers.

8. Place mark [3] on line [2] at location of last whole tile in row.

9. Place edge of carpenter's square against mark [3] to form a 90 degree angle with line [2].

10. Place board [4] against carpenter's square. Be sure that board [4] forms a 90 degree angle with line [2].

11. Fasten board [4] to floor.

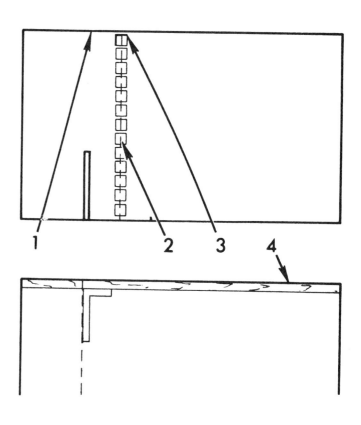

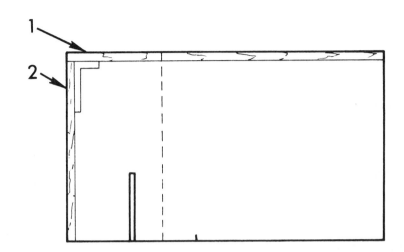

12. Place carpenter's square against board [1].

13. Place board [2] against carpenter's square. Be sure that board [2] forms a 90 degree angle with board [1].

14. Fasten board [2] to floor.

Boards [1, 2] are used as guides for laying first rows of tile.

INSTALLING A CERAMIC TILE FLOOR

▶ **Tools and Supplies**

The following tools and supplies are needed to install a ceramic tile floor:

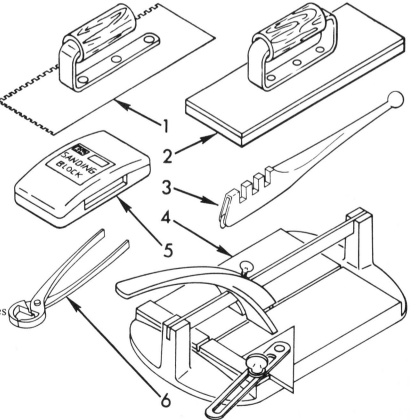

- A notched trowel [1] for applying adhesive to the floor.

- A rubber surfaced trowel [2] for applying grout to tile.

- A glass cutter [3] for scoring tiles.

- Commercial tile cutter [4] for cutting straight edges in tiles. Tile dealers have tile cutters to rent. Some will even lend tile cutters when you purchase your tile from them. Ask for operating instructions from the tile dealer.

- A sanding block [5] with 50 or 60 grit aluminum oxide coated sandpaper for smoothing cut edges of tile. Use a quality sandpaper.

- Tile nippers [6] for cutting arches or notches in tile.

- Spacers for uniformly separating all tiles.

- Rubber gloves for protecting hands when cleaning with muriatic acid.

- A sponge for removing excess grout from tiles and for cleaning with muriatic acid.

INSTALLING A CERAMIC TILE FLOOR

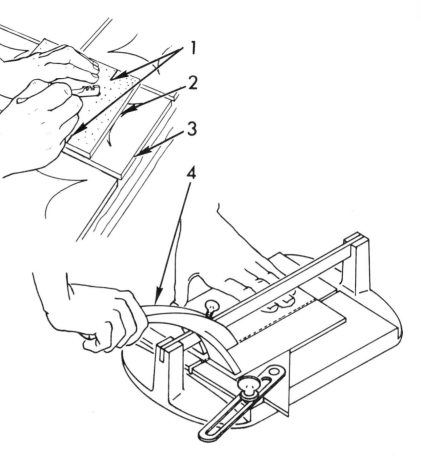

▶ **Measuring and Cutting Straight Edges**

A commercial tile cutter should be used to cut ceramic tiles. It may be rented or borrowed from a tile dealer or tool rental company. Ask dealer for instructions for using the tile cutter.

When marking a tile for cutting, always allow for 1/8-inch gap between the tile being cut and the wall or obstruction. Be sure to allow for the correct distance between the tiles.

1. Place tile [2] with glazed side down, between last installed tile [3] and wall. Place marks [1] at both edges of tile.

2. Using commercial tile cutter [4], cut tile at marked location.

3. Using aluminum oxide coated sandpaper, smooth cut edges of tile.

▶ **Measuring and Cutting Around Obstructions**

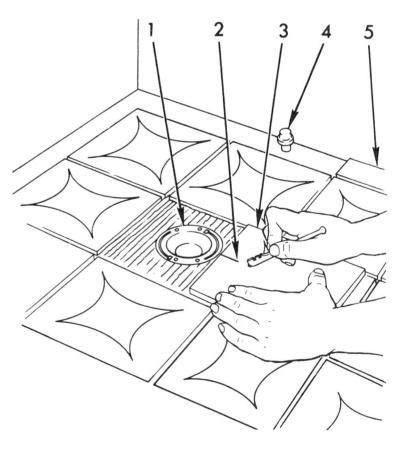

To install tile around an obstruction [1] protruding from the floor, go to Step 1.

To install tile around an obstruction [4] at a wall, you may need to cut the tile into two parts. Use the installed tile [5] next to the obstruction as a guide for cutting the piece required. After cut is made, go to Page 9, Step 3.

1. Place tile [3] against obstruction [1]. Using glass cutter, make a mark [2] on tile at center of obstruction.

2. Using commercial tile cutter, cut tile [3] into two pieces at mark [2].

8

Measuring and Cutting Around Obstructions

3. Place tile [2 or 4] against obstruction [1 or 3]. Using glass cutter, score tile at each edge of obstruction.

CAUTION

When cutting tile with tile nippers, make many small bites. Making a large bite may cause tile to crack or split.

4. Using tile nippers, cut tile [2, 4] until approximate depth and shape of obstruction is made.

5. Place tile [2, 4] against obstruction [1, 3]. Check that tile fits around obstruction.

If tile [2, 4] does not fit, repeat Steps 4 and 5.

6. Using aluminum oxide coated sandpaper, smooth cut edges of tile [2,4].

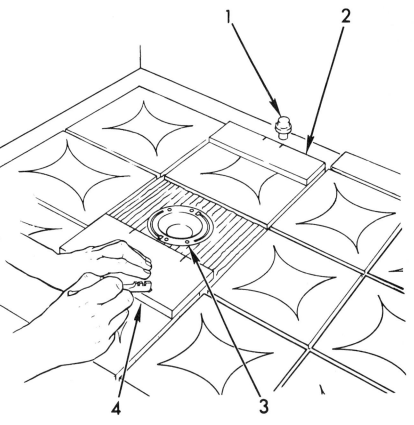

▶ **Laying Ceramic Tiles**

When laying ceramic tiles, lay all whole tiles first. After all whole tiles are laid, cut and lay pieces of tile.

To lay a ceramic tile floor, begin at the 90 degree angle formed by the two boards [2].

1. Using a notched trowel, apply adhesive to approximately 3 foot x 3 foot section of floor.

When installing tiles always lay tiles into position. Do not slide them into position. Tiles must be placed tightly against boards [2].

2. Lay first tile [1] into 90 degree angle. Press tile into adhesive.

Align remaining tiles with the first tile and boards.

Be sure to insert two spacers [3] between tiles.

3. Lay remaining whole tiles in 3 foot x 3 foot section.

4. Repeat Steps 1 through 3 until all whole tiles are laid.

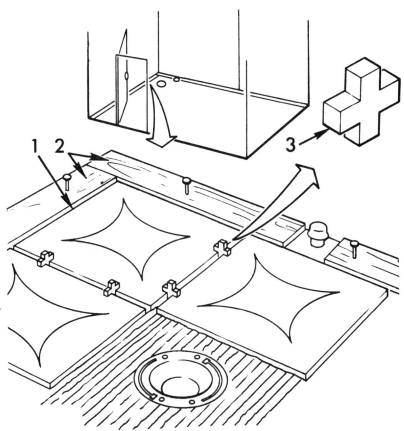

INSTALLING A CERAMIC TILE FLOOR

Laying Ceramic Tiles

Adhesive must be completely dry before the tile can be walked on. Be sure to wear clean shoes to prevent dirt from falling into spaces between tiles.

CAUTION

When removing boards [1] be careful not to move tiles. Be sure that adhesive is completely dry before removing boards.

5.   Carefully remove two boards [1].
All remaining tiles will have to be measured and cut to fit between installed tiles and wall or obstructions [2, 3].

Measure, cut, and lay tiles one at a time.

6.   Measure and cut tile [5]. Apply adhesive to back of tile.

Be sure to leave a 1/8-inch gap between wall and tile.

7.   Lay tile [5] in place. Press down firmly.

8.   Repeat Steps 5 through 7 to finish laying remaining tiles.

9.   Allow adhesive to dry for 24 hours.

10.   Remove all spacers [4].

11.   Apply grout. Page 15.

12.   Install baseboards or molding. Page 16.

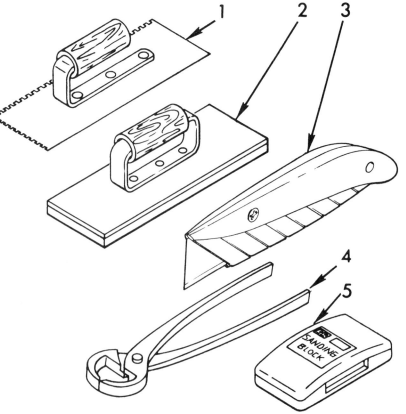

▬ INSTALLING A MOSAIC TILE FLOOR

▶ Tools and Supplies

The following tools and supplies are required:

●   A notched trowel [1] for applying adhesive to floor.

●   A rubber surfaced trowel [2] for pressing tile sheets into adhesive and for applying grout to tile.

●   A utility knife [3] for cutting through backing paper. This can either be a sharp knife or a razor blade and holder.

●   Tile nippers [4] for cutting individual ceramic tiles.

●   A sanding block [5] with 50 or 60 grit aluminum oxide coated sandpaper for smoothing cut edges of tile. Use a quality sandpaper.

●   A metal straightedge for guiding utility knife when cutting backing paper.

●   Rubber gloves for protecting hands when cleaning with muriatic acid.

●   Sponge

► **Measuring and Cutting Straight Edges**

Mosaic tile sheets are cut by cutting through the sheet and pulling the two sections apart. If the cut is made across any individual tiles, the tiles are removed from the sheet and cut and fitted individually.

When marking a sheet for cutting always allow for a 1/8-inch gap between the sheet being cut and the walls or obstructions. Gaps between sheets are approximately the same size as the gaps between individual tiles in the sheets.

1. Place sheet [3] at space between installed sheet [1] and wall. Place marks [2] at both edges of sheet.

Be sure to cut completely through paper or webbing.

2. Using utility knife and straightedge, cut completely through paper or webbing at marks [2].

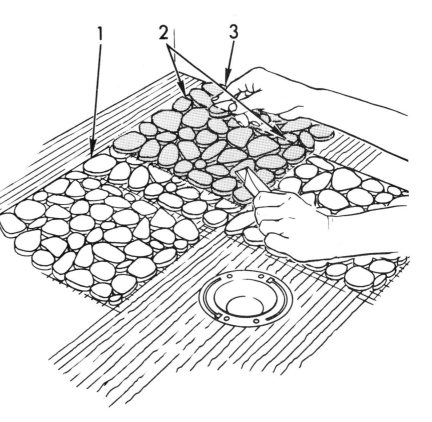

Measuring and Cutting Straight Edges

3. Carefully separate two sections of the sheet.

4. Remove any individual tiles [2] that extend beyond cut edge of sheet [1].

After sheet [1] is laid, individual tiles [2] must be cut and fitted into gaps in the sheet.

CAUTION

When cutting tile with tile nippers, make many small bites. Making a large bite may cause the tile to crack or split.

5. Using tile nippers, cut individual tiles [2] to the correct size.

6. Using aluminum oxide coated sandpaper, smooth cut edges of individual tiles.

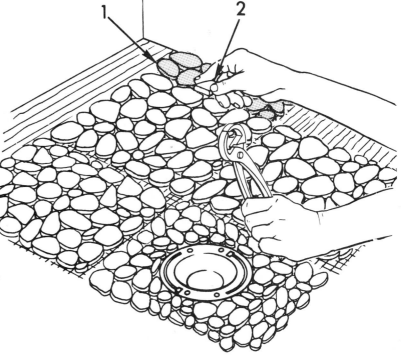

INSTALLING A MOSAIC TILE FLOOR

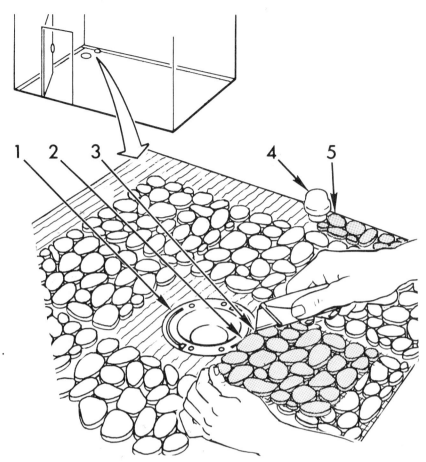

▶ **Measuring and Cutting Around Obstructions**

To install a sheet around an obstruction [1] protruding from the floor, go to Step 1.

To install a sheet around an obstruction [4] at wall, you may need to cut the sheet into two parts first. Use the installed sheet [5] next to the obstruction [4] as a guide for making the cut. After cut is made, go to Step 3, below.

1. Place sheet [2] against obstruction [1]. Place a mark [3] on sheet at center of obstruction,

2. Cut sheet [2] into two pieces at mark [3].

Measuring and Cutting Around Obstructions

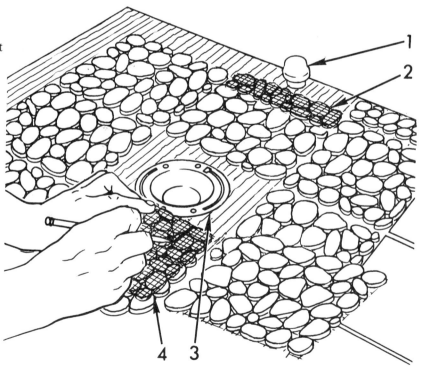

3. Place sheet [2 or 4] face side down against obstruction [1 or 3]. Place a mark on sheet at each edge of obstruction.

Be sure to cut completely through paper or webbing.

4. Using utility knife, cut sheet to approximate shape of obstruction. Carefully remove cut section.

5. Remove any whole tiles that extend beyond cut edge.

6. Place section against obstruction. Check that section fits.

If cut section does not fit, repeat Steps 4 through 6.

If first section fits, repeat Steps 3 through 6 for remaining half section of sheet.

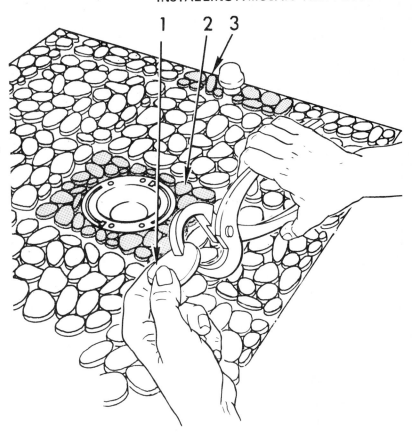

Measuring and Cutting Around Obstructions

After both sections [2 or 3] are laid, individual tiles must be cut and fitted into gaps between the sheet and the obstruction.

CAUTION

When cutting tile with tile nippers, make many small bites. Making a large bite may cause tile to crack or split.

6. Using tile nippers cut individual tiles [1] to the correct size.

7. Using aluminum oxide coated sandpaper, smooth cut edges.

▶ **Laying Mosaic Tile Sheets**

When laying mosaic tile sheets, lay all whole sheets first. After all whole sheets are laid, parts of sheets are cut and laid.

To lay a mosaic tile floor, begin at the 90 degree angle formed by the two boards [2].

1. Using notched trowel, apply adhesive to approximately 3 foot x 3 foot section of floor.

When installing sheets, always lay sheets into position. Do not slide them into position. Sheets must be placed tightly against boards [2].

2. Lay first sheet [1] into 90 degree angle. Press sheet into adhesive.

Remaining sheets are aligned with first sheet and boards.

When laying remaining sheets, make the distance between the sheets the same as the distance between the individual tiles within the sheets.

3. Lay remaining sheets in 3 foot x 3 foot section.

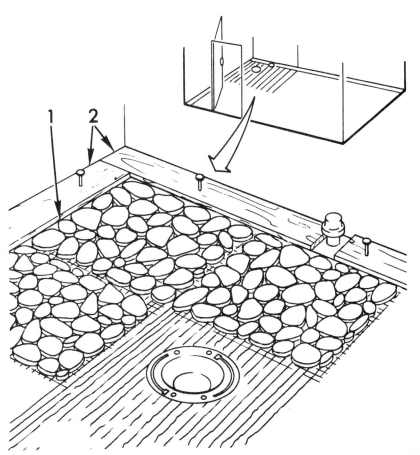

INSTALLING A MOSAIC TILE FLOOR

Laying Mosaic Tile Sheets

After each 3 foot x 3 foot area is covered, sheets must be pressed firmly into adhesive.

4. Using rubber surface trowel, press all sheets firmly into adhesive.

5. Repeat Steps 1 through 4 to lay remaining whole sheets.

Adhesive must be completely dry before the sheets can be walked on. Be sure to wear clean shoes to prevent debris from falling into spaces between tiles.

CAUTION

When removing boards [1], be careful not to move tiles. Be sure that adhesive is completely dry before removing boards.

6. Carefully remove two boards [1].

All remaining sheets will have to be measured and cut to fit between installed sheets and wall or obstruction [2, 5].

Measure, cut, and lay one sheet at a time.

7. Measure and cut sheets [3, 4]. Apply adhesive to back of sheet.

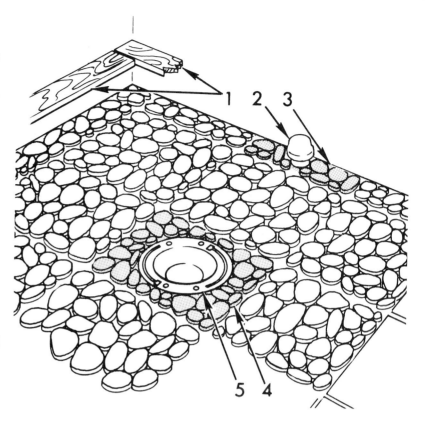

Laying Mosaic Tile Sheets

When laying sheets, make the distance between the sheet and the wall the same as the distance between the individual tiles within the sheet.

8. Lay sheet into place. Press down firmly.

9. Using rubber surfaced trowel, press sheet firmly into adhesive.

10. Repeat Steps 7 through 9 to lay remaining sheets.

11. Allow adhesive to dry for 24 hours.

12. If sheets have a protective paper coating, remove it with warm water and sponge.

13. Apply grout. Page 15.

14. Install baseboards or molding. Page 16.

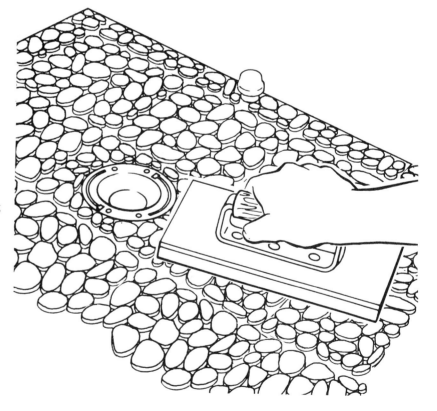

1. Mix grout according to manufacturer's instructions.

2. Using rubber surfaced trowel [1], spread grout over tile, forcing grout into all spaces.

When wiping excess grout from surface of tiles, do not remove grout from spaces between tiles.

3. Using damp sponge [2], immediately wipe excess grout from surface of tiles.

CAUTION

Grout may crack if it dries too fast. Water must be sprinkled on grout every four hours for 24 hours.

4. Allow grout to set for 24 hours before walking on floor.

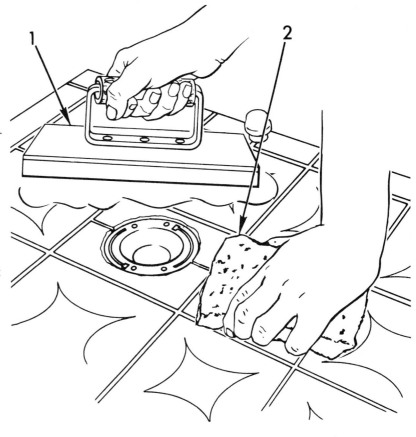

After grout has completely dried, the tiles may have a hazy film. It can be removed with a mixture of muriatic acid and water.

WARNING

Be sure to wear rubber gloves when applying muriatic acid.

5. Mix a solution of 1 part muriatic acid and 10 parts water.

6. Using sponge, wash tiles thoroughly with solution.

7. Using clean dry cloth, dry tiles completely.

INSTALLING BASEBOARDS OR MOLDING

Either wood or vinyl baseboards and molding may be used with ceramic floors.

If you plan to install vinyl cove molding [1], go to Page 34 for installation procedures.

If you plan to install wood baseboards or molding, one of the following three applications may apply to your situation.

- Install baseboard only. This application is the most common. It should be used if gap [2] between tile and wall is narrow enough to be covered by baseboard.

- Install baseboard and shoe molding. If gap [3] between tile and wall is too wide to be covered by baseboard alone, install shoe molding also.

- Install shoe molding only. If tile was installed against existing baseboard [4], shoe molding must be installed to cover any gaps.

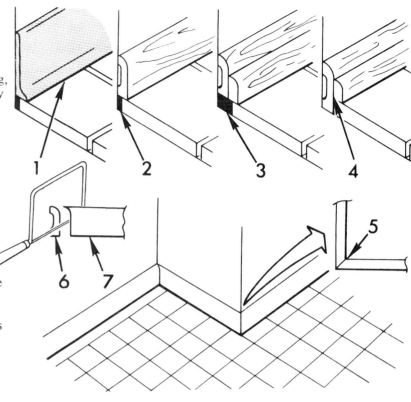

For both shoe molding and baseboards, make cuts for joints as follows:

Outside corners — use 45 degree miter cut [5]

Inside corners — use coping cut. Coping cut is made by cutting board [6] to fit closely against board [7].

REPAIRING CERAMIC TILE FLOORS

▶ **Reseating Loose Tile**

Loosening is the most common problem associated with tiles.

The following tools and supplies are required:

    Screwdriver [1]
    Putty knife [2]
    Adhesive

1. Using screwdriver, carefully remove all grout around loose tile [3].

2. Carefully insert small putty knife under tile [3] and lift out tile.

3. Remove any remaining grout from exposed edges of surrounding tiles [4] and from edges of removed tile [3].

4. Thoroughly clean all debris from exposed surface.

5. Apply tile adhesive to tile [3] according to manufacturer's instructions.

6. Install tile [3].

7. Allow to dry for 24 hours.

8. Apply grout. Page 15.

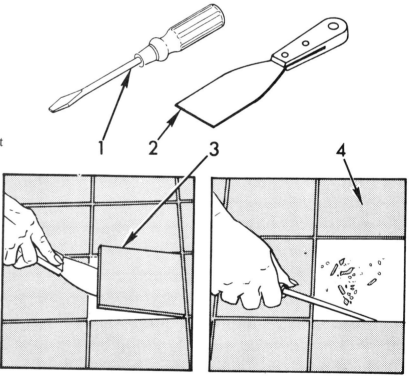

► **Replacing Damaged Tile**

When ceramic floor tiles are installed in a new home, they are usually installed over a mortar surface with thin set mortar used as an adhesive.

When the home owner installs ceramic floor tiles in his home he will install it over a wood, resilient or concrete floor. For wood and resilient floors, an adhesive is used. For concrete floors, thin set mortar is used.

The following tools and supplies are required:

    Hammer [1]
    Small chisel [2]
    Center punch [3]
    Large screwdriver [4]
    Glass cutter [5]
    Metal straightedge [6]
    Putty knife [7]
    Wooden block
    Cloth
    Thin set mortar or mastic adhesive

When replacing a cracked or chipped tile, be extremely careful not to damage the subfloor. A mortar or concrete subfloor may crack if excessive force is used when removing the tile. If the subfloor cracks, then all the tiles on the floor may be damaged.

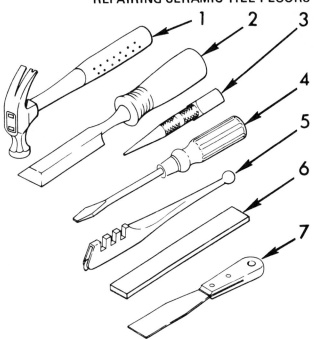

When replacing a tile originally installed with thin set mortar, use thin set mortar to replace the tile.

When replacing a tile originally installed with mastic adhesive, use mastic adhesive to replace the tile.

Replacing Damaged Tile

CAUTION

Use light taps when making hole [2] to prevent damage to subfloor.

1.   Using hammer and punch, make hole [2] in center of tile [1].

The hole [2] must be enlarged by removing small pieces from the hole. Hole should be large enough to allow a large screwdriver to be inserted.

2.   Using hammer and punch, enlarge hole [2].

If tile [1] cracks while hole is being enlarged, go to Step 4.

3.   Using glass cutter and straightedge, score tile deeply from corner to corner to form an X [3] across hole.

4.   Using screwdriver, carefully remove grout from around damaged tile.

5.   Insert screwdriver into hole. Carefully lift out sections of tile.

If sections of tile cannot be removed, hole must be enlarged.

6.   Using screwdriver, remove all remaining grout from exposed edges of surrounding tiles [4].

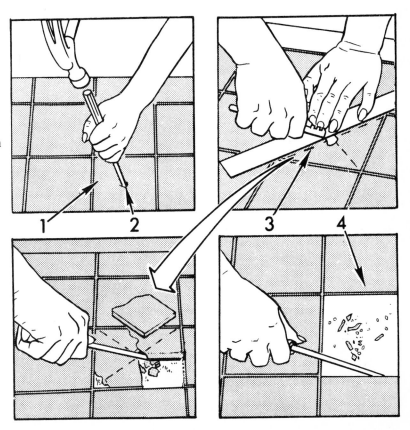

REPAIRING CERAMIC TILE FLOORS

Replacing Damaged Tile

If tile is installed with mastic adhesive, go to Step 10.

If tile is installed with thin set mortar, continue.

7. Using hammer and chisel, remove old mortar [1] to approximately 1/4-inch below bottom edge of surrounding tiles. Clean all debris from exposed surface.

8. Mix thin set mortar according to manufacturer's instruction.

9. Using putty knife, fill hole until level with mortar of surrounding tiles [2].

Go to Step 12. Read note before Step.

10. Using cloth and solvent, remove as much old adhesive as possible from exposed surface [3].

When applying adhesive, apply a thin coat of adhesive. If too much adhesive is applied, it will ooze around edges of tile.

11. Apply a thin coat of adhesive to exposed surface [3].

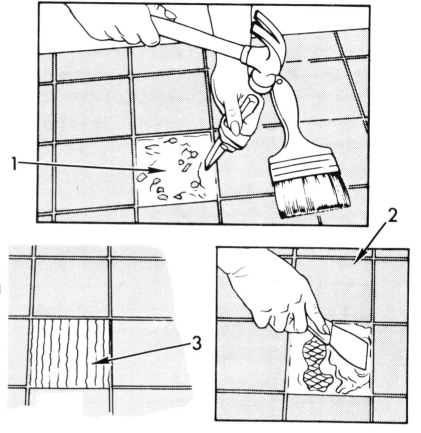

Replacing Damaged Tile

When installing new tile [1], be sure that tile is centered between installed tiles.

12. Install new tile [1].

13. Using hammer and block of wood, tap new tile until level with surrounding tiles [2].

When using thin set mortar to replace a tile, the tile may be below the level of the surrounding tiles [2]. If this happens, remove the tile and apply more thin set mortar.

After more mortar is applied, repeat Steps 12 and 13.

14. Using wet cloth, remove any thin set mortar or adhesive from surface of all tiles.

15. Allow to dry according to manufacturer's instructions.

16. Apply grout. Page 15.

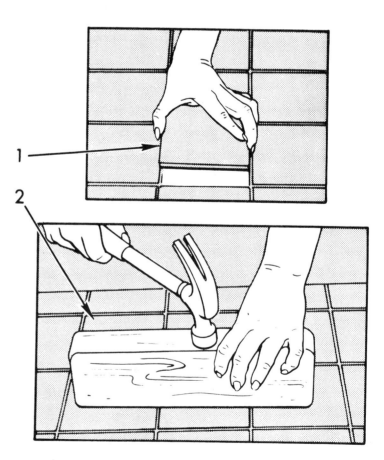

Versatile quarry tile is at home in any setting, spare or busy.

The simple quarry tile floor of this sitting room contrasts effectively with the flowered and ruffled upholstery on the invitingly cozy furniture. An unusual triangular coffee table provides a practical and artistic focus to the room. Design: Elaine Bass, ASID. Flooring: House of Quarry, Manhasset, New York. Fabric: Birge Wallcoverings. Accessories: The Nelson Rockefeller Collection. *Photo courtesy of The Nelson Rockefeller Collection.* (above)

Well planned, comfortable, and uncluttered, this family room shows a balanced arrangement of furniture for easy communication and dining. Contrasting with the warmth and brick-red color of the earthy, unglazed "Ember Flash" quarry tile floor, the rug adds an interesting texture and creates a focal point before the fireplace. The dining area is easily accessible but out of the way of the family room traffic. Design: Ian Lipton. *Photo courtesy of American Olean Tile Company.* (left)

Tile is a beautiful alternative for living and dining areas.

The deep brown of "Encore Seal" ceramic tile provides a handsome, easy-care backdrop to this elegant dining table and chairs set against an Oriental screen. Design: Kitty Hawk, Inc., Fort Worth, Texas. *Photo courtesy of American Olean Tile Company*. (facing page, top left)

The same "Encore Seal" tile used in the dining room at left works equally well in this family/television room. The contrast between the textures of the floor, coffee tables, and fabrics enhances each of them. Design: Kitty Hawk, Inc., Fort Worth, Texas. *Photo courtesy of American Olean Tile Company*. (facing page, top right)

A ceramic tile foyer leads to the dining area and gracefully accents the enclosed atrium and sunken living room, setting the mood for a casually elegant lifestyle. "Encore Sand" is a mellow, matte glazed tile that offers increased slip resistance. Builder: Baywood Design and Construction Company, Winter Park, Florida. *Photo courtesy of American Olean Tile Company*. (facing page, bottom)

A comfortable, sunny corner works equally well as an office-at-home or a serving area for parties. A handsome, muted pattern made by combining "Flint" and "Hearth" ceramic tiles adds a rich, yet practical look. Floor Design: Philadelphia Design. *Photo courtesy of American Olean Tile Company*. (right)

This beautifully outfitted craft room, a weaver's paradise, features a handsome, totally practical ceramic tile floor. The "Birch" tiles could serve equally well in a living or dining room. *Photo courtesy of American Olean Tile Company*. (below)

Tiles make a decorative, easy-care surface for kitchens and patios.

A mellow "Encore Camel" ceramic tile floor ties this kitchen and dining area together. The island counter provides a convenient work area for food and drink preparation. The countertop is easy-to-clean "Tuscany Almond" textured ceramic tile. Builder: Baywood Design and Construction Company, Inc., Winter Park, Florida. *Photo courtesy of American Olean Tile Company.* (left)

This country kitchen proves that old-fashioned good looks are possible today, with a little Yankee ingenuity. Coordinating wallcovering and fabrics provide both authentic Early American decor and warm color accents to be picked up throughout the room. Underfoot, the ceramic flooring is easy to clean, easy to live with, and hard to beat for downright beauty. Design: Margot Gunther, ASID. Flooring: Italian Tile Import Corporation. Furniture: SK Products Corporation. Wallcoverings and Fabric: Birge Wallcoverings. Accessory (wooden soldier whirligig): The Nelson Rockefeller Collection. *Photo courtesy of SK Products Corporation.* (below)

What better way to enhance lovely wood cabinetry than with warm, gently textured "Tuscany Gold Hexagon" ceramic tile walls and countertops. The floor design is especially interesting, incorporating the same hexagonal tile inlaid in a rich, warm grid pattern. *Photo courtesy of American Olean Tile Company.* (above left)

Mineral composition tiles from Z-BRICK are an attractive, easy-to-install flooring alternative. The kitchen is tiled with "Desert Tan Rustic Paver," and the spacious patio features rugged-looking "Old Georgian Floor Brick." The brick-look tiles are durable, fire-safe, and colorfast. *Photo courtesy of Z-BRICK Company.* (above right)

Small-unit ceramic mosaics lend themselves to infinite design possibilities. The pattern on this patio is an extension of the indoor flooring shown on the back cover of this book. The impervious tiles used on both the floor and benches is suitable for exterior as well as interior use. *Photo courtesy of American Olean Tile Company.* (below right)

The most opulent bathrooms gleam with tile.

The elegantly geometric lines of this bath are enhanced by a band of color graduating from deep blue to soft gray. A well-chosen plant adds softness. The rugged unglazed surface of the white porcelain ceramic mosaics makes them ideal for baths and other wet areas. Builder: Chaparral Builders, Apple Valley, California. *Photo courtesy of American Olean Tile Company.* (above left)

A Roman tub with circulation jets dominates this spacious bath. The step around the tub and the shelf at wall end provide room for bath accessories. The tile, a deep orange, adds drama to an already luxurious bath. For contrast, the floor tile has been installed in a basketweave pattern. Tile Contractor: A.B. Tile Company, San Mateo, California. *Photo courtesy of American Olean Tile Company.* (above right)

A long, ceramic-tile vanity, illuminated by domed skylights and recessed ceiling lights, provides space for cosmetic needs and storage. The dressing area is carpeted, but the tub/shower area is tiled with a slip-resistant, unglazed tile. Design: Kitty Hawk Design, Arlington, Texas. Tub: Kohler's Expresso. *Photo courtesy of American Olean Tile Company.* (left)

24

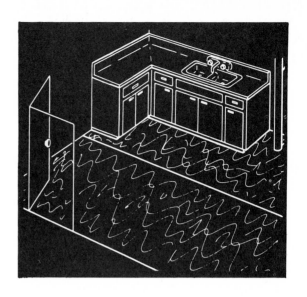

RESILIENT FLOORS

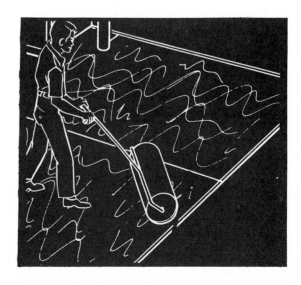

The term resilient floors applies to many different types of flooring. The following are the most common types of resilient floor materials:

- Vinyl asbestos tile
- Vinyl tile
- Asphalt tile
- Vinyl sheet flooring
- Linoleum

Resilient floors are very popular for use in nearly all rooms in your home. There is a wide variety of colors, patterns and textures available.

Before selecting the type of resilient floor for your specific needs, you should become familiar with the characteristics of each type, as well as advantages and disadvantages of both tile and sheet installations.

In kitchens and bathrooms, or around a bar where frequent water spillage is expected, consider installing sheet flooring rather than tile. Regardless of how tightly tiles are butted together, a certain amount of water will seep into the seams. This can cause loosening of the tiles, as well as promote conditions for growth of mold and fungus.

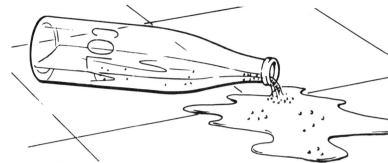

Resilient floors are generally installed with some type of adhesive. Self-sticking tiles are available which require no adhesive. Some sheet flooring also requires no adhesive.

Tiles are commonly available in sizes of 9 in. x 9 in. and 12 in. x 12 in. Sheet flooring is available in widths from 6 to 12 feet. Sheets can be cut to any length desired when you make your purchase.

Sheet flooring results in much fewer seams than tiles. No seams at all are required where one sheet is large enough to do the job. Additionally, seam sealing compounds are available for some types of vinyl sheet flooring. They seal the seams completely, preventing the problems inherent in a tile installation.

Resilient floors are available in smooth or textured patterns. These differences should also be considered because of varying maintenance requirements.

Textured floors present more maintenance problems than smooth floors. Dirt and wax build up in recessed areas of textured patterns. Smooth floors require less scrubbing. Generally only light mopping is required.

The ability of the floor to resist indentations is also an important consideration. Based solely on patterns, a textured pattern is best where heavy furniture is located. Textured floors will hide indentations better than smooth floors. However, with either type furniture leg cups are recommended to minimize indentations.

The following paragraphs describe characteristics of each type of resilient floor material which you should be aware of before making a selection.

► **Vinyl Asbestos Tile**

Vinyl asbestos tiles are made by binding asbestos filler between outside layers of vinyl.

Vinyl asbestos tiles will last indefinitely under normal wear and with normal maintenance. Although they resist indentations better than other resilient tiles, they are generally less resistant to abrasion and household chemicals than solid vinyl tiles.

Both self-sticking tiles and tiles which require separate adhesive for installation are available. Consider installing self-sticking tiles because of their ease of installation.

▶ Vinyl Tiles

Most solid vinyl tiles have inlaid patterns and colors which extend throughout the entire thickness. Because of this, vinyl tiles are very hard to wear away, making them the most durable of the resilient floors.

Vinyl tiles are one of the quietest and most comfortable resilient floor materials, although they are less resistant to indentations than vinyl asbestos tiles.

▶ Asphalt Tiles

Asphalt tiles are less durable than other types of resilient tiles. They have a grainy surface which can be penetrated easily by grease and oil. Because of the advantages of vinyl asbestos and solid vinyl tiles, asphalt is not installed in many areas of the home today.

▶ Vinyl Sheet Flooring

Vinyl sheet flooring is by far the most popular resilient material available in sheet form.

Vinyl sheets are made with a vinyl layer on top of an asbestos or felt backing material. The asbestos backing is suitable for installation in any area of the home. Felt backing must be used on wood frame floors only.

A cushioned sheet flooring is also available. A layer of resilient material is pressed between the top vinyl layer and the backing material.

Noncushioned sheet flooring has nearly the same characteristics as the vinyl tiles.

Cushioned sheet flooring is generally more durable than noncushioned. It is very quiet and comfortable to walk on, but has less resistance to indentations than the noncushioned type.

▶ Linoleum

Linoleum has limited use in most homes today. It can be more expensive than the vinyls, yet less durable. Additionally, the variety of colors and patterns is less than other resilient flooring.

Linoleum's resistance to moisture, grease and oil is good, but resistance to alkalies is poor.

▶ Vinyl Cove Molding

Vinyl cove molding [1] is an attractive alternative to standard baseboards and molding. It is available in many colors and designs. Whether you select matching or contrasting colors is a matter of personal preference.

Both self-sticking types and types which require a separate adhesive are available. Note that the adhesive used to install cove molding is not the same as that used to install tiles and sheet flooring. A special adhesive is required for holding to vertical wall surfaces.

Vinyl cove molding is easy to install. Most is in standard 4-foot sections. Pre-shaped inside and outside corners are available. The coved bottom edge is superior to standard molding for keeping floors sanitary.

Resilient tiles and sheet flooring may be installed on the following surfaces:

- Wood
- Concrete
- Resilient

Because a resilient floor is flexible and tends to take the shape of the subfloor surface, the floor surface must be smooth and clean. Any surface irregularities may be visible after installation of your new floor.

Before checking the floor surface, remove shoe moldings or baseboards in the area to be covered. They will be installed after your new floor is complete.

If installing vinyl cove molding instead of base-boards or shoe molding, it is best to check the baseboard area at this time. Because adhesive is required, area should be smooth and clean.

Before beginning to install a resilient floor, carefully check the floor and make any necessary repairs.

▶ **Checking a Wood Floor**

A wood floor must be firm, even, and clean before resilient floors can be installed.

It is recommended that you do not lay resilient floors directly over plank or strip flooring. An underlayment grade of plywood, particle board, or hardboard should be installed.

1. Check that floor is firm and does not move or flex.

If floor is not firm, it must be made firm.

2. Check the floor for the following problems:

    - Protruding nails
    - Loose boards
    - High or low spots
    - Cracks or gaps

If any problems are found, they must be repaired.

3. Clean entire floor area thoroughly.

▶ **Checking a Concrete Floor**

A concrete floor must be level, clean, and sealed before resilient floors can be installed.

1. Check the floor for the following problems:
    - High or low spots
    - Cracks or gaps
    - Moisture

If any problems are found, they must be repaired.

2. Clean floor surface to remove all oil, dirt, and grease.

Floor must be sealed to provide a good moisture barrier between concrete and resilient floors. Check with your dealer for the type of sealer to use.

3. Seal floor.

▶ **Checking a Resilient Floor**

A resilient floor must be even, securely installed, and clean before a new resilient floor can be installed over it.

It is sometimes recommended to remove the old floor completely. Resilient tiles or sheet flooring can become loose in time, resulting in damage to the new floor covering.

If removing old resilient floor, be sure to remove, or at least smooth, old adhesive before installing your new floor.

If installing resilient floor over old resilient floor, perform Steps 1 and 2.

1. Check the floor for the following problems:

    - Loose tiles, sheets or pieces
    - Cracks or holes

If any problems are found, they must be repaired.

A commercial wax remover should be used to remove all old wax from the floor.

2. Remove all old wax from floor.

▶ Planning and Estimating

Install a tile floor in the following sequence:

- Determine the pattern, color and size of the tiles. This is entirely your own preference.

- Remove shoe moldings or baseboards.

- Estimate the amount of materials needed. See below.

- Obtain any needed tools and supplies. Page 30.

- Check the floor surface. Page 28.

- Square off the floor. Page 30.

- Lay tiles. Page 32.

- Install baseboards or molding. Page 44. If installing vinyl cove molding, go to Page 34.

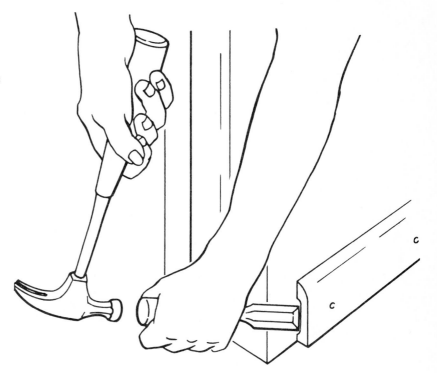

Planning and Estimating

To estimate the amount of materials needed, you should make a detailed sketch of the floor to be covered. Graph paper is very handy for making this sketch.

Measure and record all dimensions on the sketch.

Take the sketch to a tile dealer. He will help you determine the following:

- Number of tiles needed
- Amount of adhesive needed
- Amount of cove molding and adhesive, if required.

Purchase more tiles than will actually be used. They will be useful in case of mistakes or for future repairs.

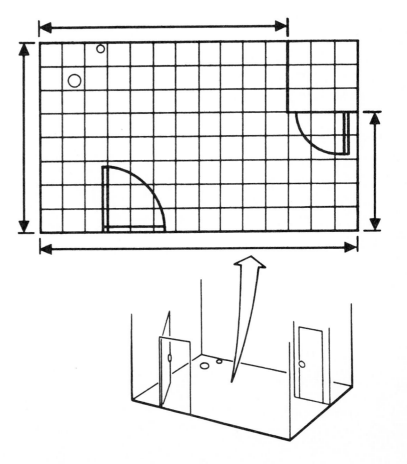

INSTALLING TILE FLOORS

▶ Tools and Supplies

The following tools and supplies are required to install tile floors:

- A tape measure [1] for making required measurements

- A chalk line [2] for squaring off the floor

- A sharp utility knife [3] or linoleum knife for cutting tiles. Some tile materials can be cut with scissors.

- A metal straightedge [4] for guiding knife when cutting tiles

- A notched trowel [5] for applying adhesive. Some adhesives can be applied with a paintbrush. Check manufacturer's instructions.

- Linoleum roller [6] or rolling pin [7] for pressing tiles firmly in place. Linoleum roller can be rented from most tool rental dealers.

- Clean rags for wiping excess adhesive from tiles

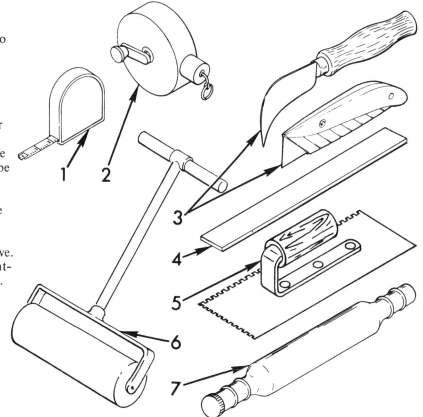

▶ Squaring Off the Floor

Chalk lines [2, 4] must be marked to provide a guide for laying tiles squarely on the floor.

1. Locate the center of two side walls. Place marks [1, 3] on the floor at each center.

2. Attach chalk line to mark [1]. Pull chalk line to mark [3].

3. Pull chalk line tight between marks [1, 3]. Pull line straight up from floor. Release chalk line.

Chalk line will mark a straight line [2] on the floor.

4. Repeat Steps 1 through 3 to make chalk line [4] between two end walls.

Narrow tiles along the borders of the floor are less attractive than wider tiles. To prevent having narrow tiles along the borders, chalk lines [2, 4] may have to be adjusted. Go to Page 31 to determine width of border tiles.

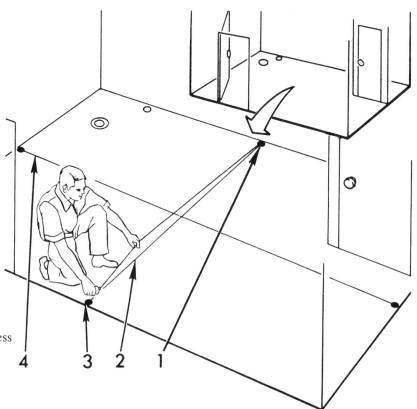

Squaring Off the Floor

Rows [2] of loose tiles are used to determine width of tiles along borders.

5. Beginning where chalk lines [1] cross, lay tiles in two rows [2] as shown.

If distance between last tiles [3, 4] and wall is half-tile width or more, chalk lines do not need adjusting. Go to Page 32 to lay tiles.

If distance is less than a half-tile width, rows must be adjusted and new chalk lines marked.

6. Adjust rows [7] until distance between last tiles [8, 9] and wall is at least a half-tile width.

7. Using rows [7] as a guide, make two chalk lines [5] parallel to old chalk lines [6].

Chalk lines [5] will be used as the guide for laying tiles.

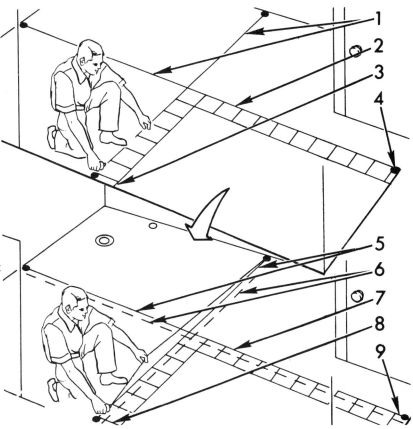

▶ **Measuring and Cutting Border Tiles**

After all whole tiles in a section [1] have been laid, measure and cut the tiles for the borders [2]. Each border tile is measured and cut individually.

The following procedures show how to measure and mark a border tile quickly and accurately.

1. Place a loose tile [4] on top of the last whole tile [3] in any row. Align edges of tiles [3,4]. Be sure that tile [4] is facing up and that its design matches tile [3] exactly.

2. Place a tile [5] on top of tile [4]. Hold one edge of tile [5] firmly against wall.

3. Using edge of tile [5] as a guide, make a mark [6] on tile [4].

4. Remove tile [4] from floor.

Before cutting entirely through tile [4], first make a light cut along mark [6] to guide knife.

5. While firmly holding metal straightedge along mark [6], cut tile [4] with sharp knife. Piece [7] of tile will fit into border closely and accurately.

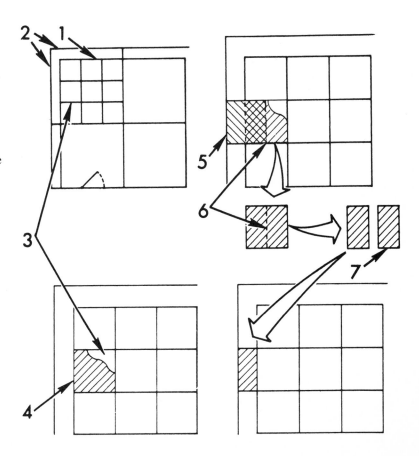

INSTALLING TILE FLOORS

▶ Measuring and Cutting Around Obstructions

Measuring and cutting around an obstruction generally requires making a paper pattern of the desired shape. The pattern is then transferred to the tile for cutting.

Whole tiles [1] may require cutting into two sections to fit around posts or other obstructions.

Border tiles [2] may need a pattern. Make slit [3] as shown to fit around pipes.

If possible, the obstruction should be removed to prevent irregular cuts. For example, a toilet should be removed and the tiles laid under it. This will insure a good appearance at the toilet base after it is installed.

When tracing the pattern on the tile, plan your cut so that patterns match between tiles.

A sharp utility knife is used to cut tiles. A first, light cut is helpful in guiding the knife during the next deep cut.

Use a metal straightedge as a guide for straight cuts. A can or other rounded object of the right size can be used as a guide for curved cuts.

▶ Laying Tiles

Floor must be squared off. Page 30.
Read through entire procedure before beginning to lay tiles.

Tiles are laid in one section [2] at a time. Both whole tiles and border tiles are laid before tiling the next section.

Begin in the section [2] farthest away from the entryway to the room. Plan to finish at the entryway.

If installing self-sticking tiles, no adhesive is required. Go to Page 33.

Application of adhesive may vary depending on manufacturer. Some adhesive can be applied with a paintbrush [4]. Others require spreading with a notched trowel [3]. Read manufacturer's instructions for the proper method of application.

When applying adhesive, be careful not to cover chalk lines [1].

1. Apply an even coat of adhesive to one entire section [2]. Allow adhesive to set up according to manufacturer's instructions.

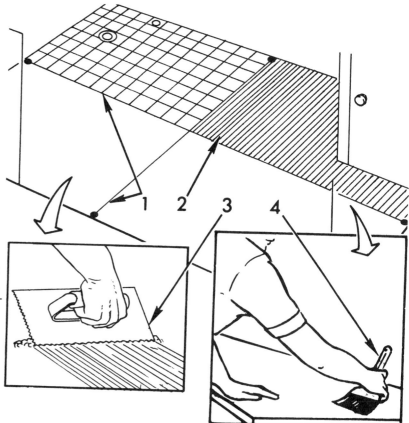

Laying Tiles

Self-sticking tiles and tiles which require adhesive are both laid in the sequence as shown. First tile [1] is laid where chalk lines [2] cross. Remaining tiles are butted tightly against adjacent tiles.

Do not slide tiles into position. Try to place them in their correct position the first time. Plan the layout of patterned tiles before installation.

As tiles are pressed into place, adhesive may be forced onto the surface of the tiles. Have a damp rag handy to wipe off excess adhesive before it dries.

You may have to stand or kneel on laid tiles to complete a section. Be careful not to move them out of position.

Lay all whole tiles [1] first. Tile around any obstructions in the middle of the section. Then go back and fit tiles around the obstruction. Page 32 describes how to measure and cut around obstructions.

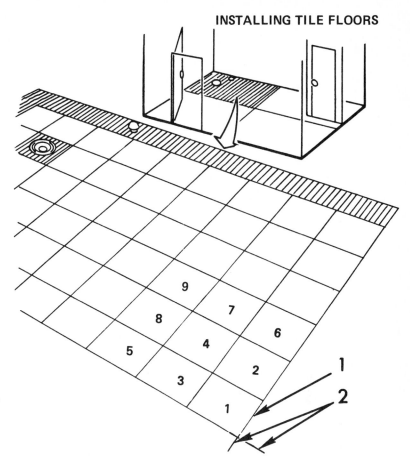

Laying Tiles

2. Following the sequence as shown, lay all whole tiles [1]. Press each tile firmly over its entire surface as it is laid.

Border tiles [2] are cut and laid one at a time. Page 31 describes how to measure and cut border tiles.

3. Cut and lay border tiles [2].

4. Using a linoleum roller or rolling pin, press down all tiles [1, 2] in the section.

5. Repeat Pages 32 through 33 to lay tiles in remaining sections.

After entire floor is tiled, baseboards or molding must be installed. Page 44.

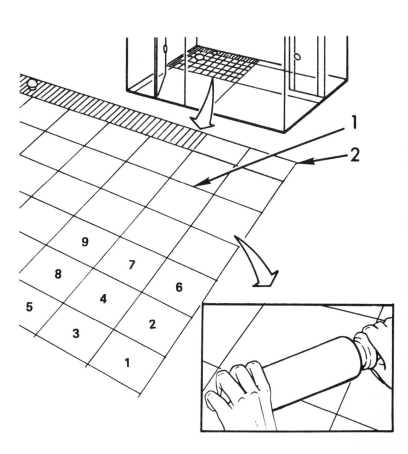

INSTALLING TILE FLOORS

▶ Installing Vinyl Cove Molding

Vinyl cove molding [1] is an attractive way to finish off your floor. Sections of vinyl molding are easy to handle and easy to install.

The wall surface along baseboard areas must be smooth, clean, and dry.

The following tools and supplies are required to install vinyl cove molding:

- A tape measure [2] for making required measurements

- A sharp utility knife [3] for cutting molding. Some vinyl material can be cut with scissors.

- A metal straightedge [4] for guiding knife when cutting molding

- Molding adhesive. Your flooring dealer will recommend the type, and the tools required for its application.

- Clean rags for wiping excess adhesive from molding.

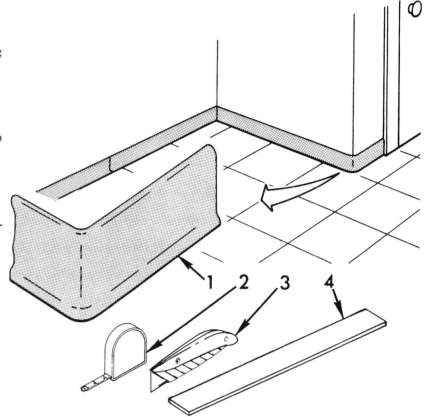

Installing Vinyl Cove Molding

The adhesive used to install vinyl molding must be made specifically for vertical surface applications. Adhesive used to install flooring is not recommended.

Application of adhesive may vary depending on manufacturer. Most adhesive is applied with a narrow paintbrush or notched trowel. Read manufacturer's instructions for proper method of application.

Apply even coats of adhesive in strips [1] along the base of the wall. Place a section of molding [2] at installed position to determine the required area of coverage. Allow adhesive to set up according to manufacturer's instructions.

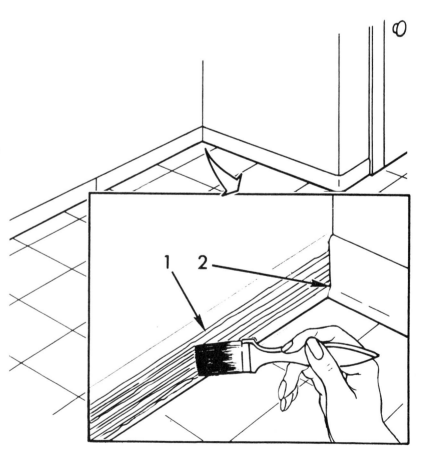

Installing Vinyl Cove Molding

Begin installing sections of molding [2] at an inside corner [1]. Butt sections tightly against each other. Press each section firmly against the wall and floor.

If adhesive spreads onto areas not to be covered, have a damp rag handy to wipe off excess immediately.

At outside corners [7], stretch molding [6] tightly around corner. Press it firmly against wall and floor.

At inside corners [3], molding can be cut to fit. Ends of sections [4, 5] can be mitered for a better fit than just butting ends together. A sharp utility knife or scissors is used to cut molding.

Another method used at inside corners [3] is to make a cut part way through the back of one section of molding at the location of the corner. Molding is then bent to fit snugly into the corner. Make cut carefully with a sharp utility knife. Be sure not to cut through front surface of molding.

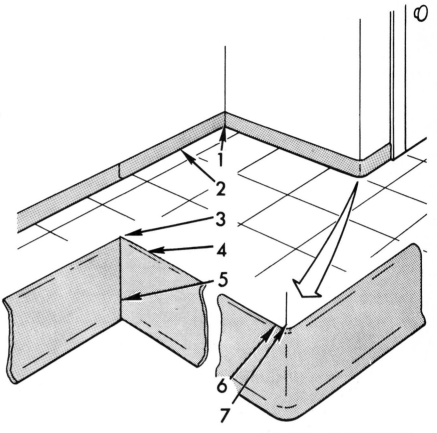

INSTALLING SHEET FLOORS

▶ **Planning and Estimating**

Install a sheet floor in the following sequence:

- Plan your job and estimate the amount of materials needed. Page 36.

- Obtain any needed tools and supplies. Page 38.

- Remove shoe moldings or baseboards.

- Check the floor surface. Page 28.

- Lay sheet flooring. Page 38.

- Install baseboards or molding. Page 44. If installing vinyl cove molding, go to Page 34.

INSTALLING SHEET FLOORS

Planning and Estimating

Proper planning is an important first step in installing sheet floors. Planning enables you to do the job with a minimum amount of time, money and materials.

Several factors should be considered before selecting the sheet flooring.

Sheet flooring is commonly available in widths of 6 to 12 feet. Materials can be cut to any length when you make your purchase. Because of the varied widths, many rooms can be done with one sheet cut to the appropriate length.

If your floor requires more than one sheet, plan the position of each sheet for the fewest number of seams. The fewer the number of seams, the easier the job will be. If possible, plan the position of each sheet so that seams are not in a dominant or heavy-traffic area of the floor.

When more than one sheet is required, sheets of different manufactured widths should not be mixed. Colors between sheets of different widths may not exactly match. For example, do not purchase a 6-foot width and 9-foot width to cover a 15-foot floor. Combine widths of the same roll to cover your floor.

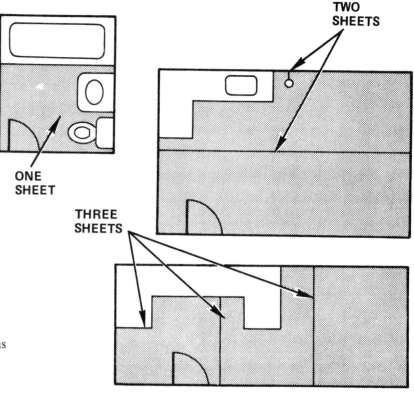

ONE SHEET

TWO SHEETS

THREE SHEETS

Planning and Estimating

The variety of designs for sheet flooring is almost unlimited. Some designs are repeated at regular intervals and require matching. Other designs are randomly spaced and require no matching. You should consider this feature when selecting your floor covering. If two or more sheets are needed for your floor, consider a design which requires no matching. It is easier to install and will result in less wasted material.

The cutting of sheet flooring to fit an area is sometimes difficult without first making a pattern out of paper. Patterns are recommended in rooms requiring only one sheet of flooring [1] and for any area of a room where a sheet must be cut to fit around obstructions [2].

Patterns are not generally required for complete lengths of flooring [3] which cover an unobstructed area with no irregularities.

The best material for pattern making is building paper or felt paper. Both are sturdy enough to be cut to exact dimensions as a guide for cutting each sheet. See Page 42 for procedures for making a pattern.

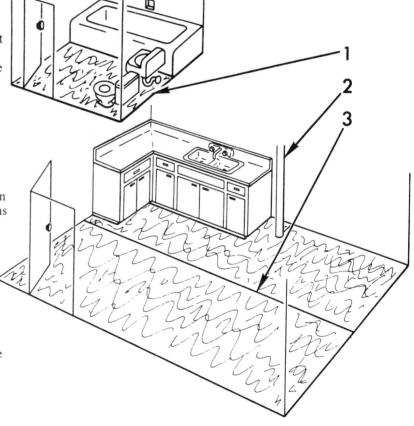

1

2

3

Planning and Estimating

All removable obstructions on the floor should
be removed before installing the flooring. In a
bathroom, you may even want to remove the
toilet to prevent having to make irregular cuts
around its base. An area of the sheet can be cut
to fit the opening and the border around the
toilet will be smooth and even.

The type of sheet flooring you select generally
determines whether or not adhesive is required to
attach sheets to your floor. Some types require
no adhesive. For others, adhesive is recommended, either over the entire floor surface or
along edges and seams of each sheet.

Your flooring dealer will recommend the type of
adhesive for your situation and its application.
Aerosol adhesives and double-face tape are some
of the various methods which can be used to
secure flooring.

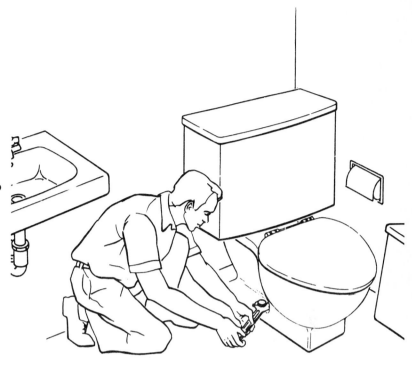

Planning and Estimating

Seam sealing compounds are available for some
types of flooring. They fuse the seams of flooring together to make a solid surface with no
cracks or gaps. If your installation has seams,
consider using a sealer. It will make the seams
less noticeable if not invisible. It can also be
used to make mistakes in cutting and joining less
obvious.

To finish off the floor, you will probably want to
install a metal threshhold [1] at entryways into
the room. Vinyl cove molding [2], available in
matching colors and designs, can be installed as
an attractive alternative to standard baseboards
and shoe moldings.

The best method of estimating the amount of
materials needed and to verify your plans for
installation is to make a detailed sketch of the
floor. A piece of graph paper is handy for making
the sketch.

Measure and record floor dimensions on your
sketch. Be sure to include all obstructions on the
floor. Take the sketch to a flooring dealer. He
will help you determine the type and quantity of
materials needed to do the job.

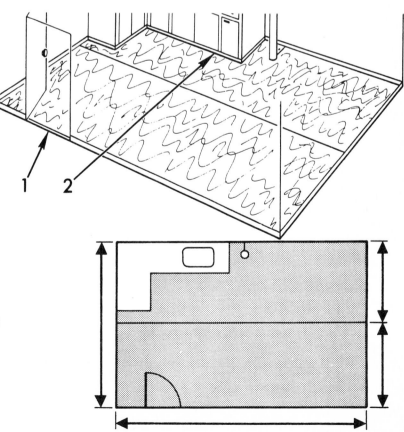

INSTALLING SHEET FLOORS

▶ Tools and Supplies

The following tools and supplies are required to install sheet floors:

- A tape measure [1] for making required measurements

- Building paper [2] or felt paper for making patterns

- A sharp utility knife [3] for cutting sheet flooring. Some types can be cut with scissors.

- A metal straightedge [4] for guiding knife

- Linoleum roller [5] or rolling pin for pressing the flooring into adhesive. Roller can be rented from most tool rental dealers.

- Adhesive. Your flooring dealer will recommend the type, method of application, and tools required to apply adhesive.

- Sheet flooring

- Seam sealing compound if required for your type of flooring.

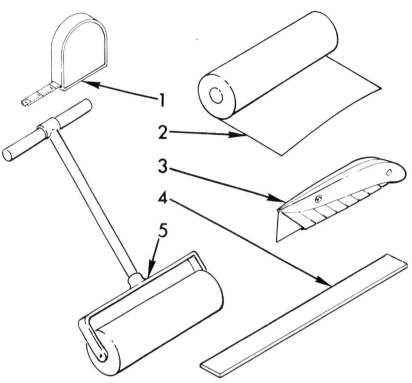

- Metal threshholds as required

- Clean cloth for wiping up excess adhesive

▶ Laying Sheet Flooring

Read through entire discussion and procedures before beginning to lay sheet flooring.

Floor surface must be checked. Page 28.

Sheet flooring is cut and installed one sheet at a time. After a sheet [3] is cut to fit, adhesive is applied to the floor. Some types of flooring may not require adhesive. Your dealer will be able to give you this information when you make your purchase.

The sheet [3] is then laid into the adhesive, and the sequence is repeated for second and successive sheets [1].

In most cases, laying sheet flooring is a two-man job. A helper can always be useful, especially if working with large widths of flooring.

Use your floor sketch as a guide during installation. For rooms requiring more than one sheet, the first sheet installed is usually along the longest or most regular wall [4].

If more than one sheet is to be installed, seams [2] must be made. Read instructions for making seams on Page 40 before continuing.

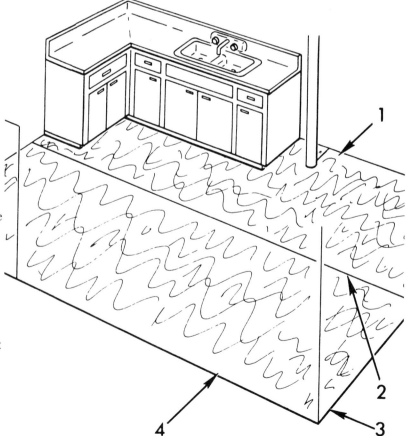

38

Laying Sheet Flooring

Each sheet must fit snugly around obstructions [1] and at edges not to be covered by baseboards or molding. A 1/8-inch gap [3] must be left along walls to allow for expansion of the floor and walls.

When cutting sheets, be sure to consider flooring designs. Plan where you want designs to end at walls. If installing more than one sheet, plan accordingly so that designs will match when second and successive sheets are overlapped and the seams [2] double cut.

Page 42 describes cutting sheets from a pattern. Follow these instructions for rooms requiring only one sheet and for sheets requiring irregular cuts around obstructions.

Page 43 describes cutting sheets without a pattern. Follow these instructions only when the sheet covers a regular shape with no obstructions.

After cutting the sheet to fit, continue.

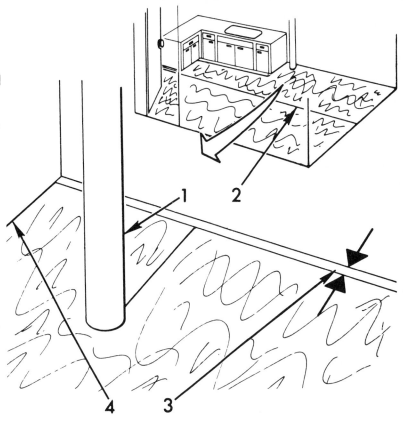

Laying Sheet Flooring

1. Move cut sheet [2] to installed position with a 1/8-inch gap [1] along walls.

2. Roll up half the sheet [2].

CAUTION

If seams are to be made, remember to apply adhesive [3] only to within 6 to 8 inches of seam area [4].

3. Following manufacturer's instructions for method of application and set up time, apply adhesive [3] to uncovered half of section.

4. Roll sheet [2] over adhesive [3], keeping 1/8-inch gap [5] along walls.

5. Immediately after moving sheet [6] over adhesive, press sheet firmly over entire surface with linoleum roller or rolling pin. Work from the center to the edges to remove any trapped air.

6. Using a damp cloth, wipe up any excess adhesive.

7. Repeat Steps 2 through 6 to lay second half of sheet [2].

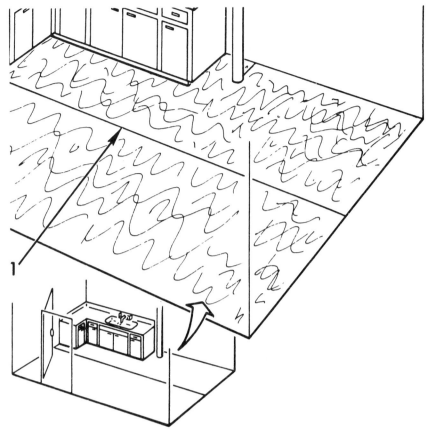

Laying Sheet Flooring

8. If second and successive sheets are to be laid, repeat Page 39 to lay each sheet. Be sure to read instructions for making seams, below, before cutting and laying sheets.

9. Make seams [1] if required. See below.

10. Install shoe moldings or baseboards, Page 44. If installing vinyl cove molding, see Page 34 for installation instructions.

11. Install metal threshholds at entryways if desired.

▶ **Making Seams**

To conceal joints between two or more sheets, seams must be carefully cut to fit.

When two or more sheets [1, 2] are laid, the second and successive sheets must be installed with an overlap [3]. The overlap is then double cut to make a tightly fitting seam.

1. Lay first sheet [2] by following the instructions beginning on Page 38. Be sure to apply adhesive [4] no closer than 6 to 8 inches from the overlap [3]. There must be no adhesive under seam area when cutting.

CAUTION

When cutting and laying remaining sheets [1], be sure to match designs as required. Many types of sheet flooring designs require reversing the direction of each successive sheet to obtain a match.

For designs requiring no match, overlap [3] is approximately 1/4 inch. For designs which require matching, overlap is increased by whatever amount it takes to match designs.

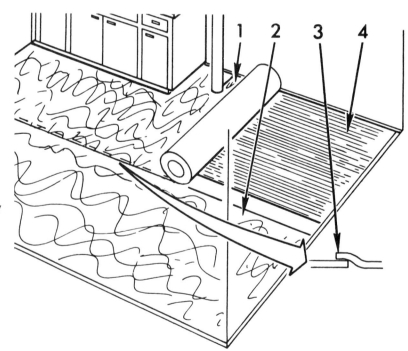

2. Lay remaining sheets [1] as in Step 1, making sure to overlap sheets and match designs if required.

After all sheets [1, 2] are laid, seams can be made. Go to Page 41.

Making Seams

CAUTION

For making seams, cutting strokes must be firm enough to cut through both layers of overlap [1]. Make all cuts in the same direction. Utility knife must be held straight up and down so that edges of cut are square.

For geometric designs, make cut along edge of design. For designs requiring no match, make cut at center of overlap [1].

3. Using straightedge and one firm stroke with utility knife, cut through overlap [1].

4. Carefully remove strips [2, 3] from top and bottom sheet.

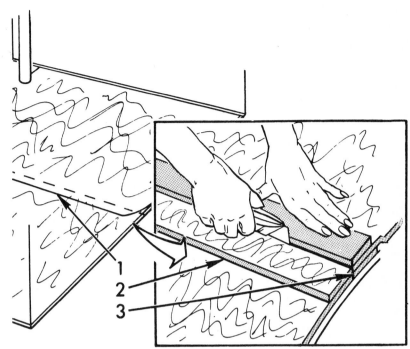

Making Seams

Do not use an excessive amount of adhesive along seam area [3]. This will prevent a large amount of seepage when seams are rolled.

5. Fold back edges of sheets [2, 4]. Apply adhesive to floor along seam.

6. Carefully place edges of sheets [2, 4] firmly into adhesive.

7. Using linoleum roller or rolling pin, press sheets [2, 4] firmly over entire seam area [3]. Have a damp cloth handy to remove any excess adhesive.

8. Repeat Steps 3 through 7 to make all remaining seams.

9. Apply seam sealing compound along all seams [1] if it can be used for your flooring. Follow manufacturer's instructions for its application.

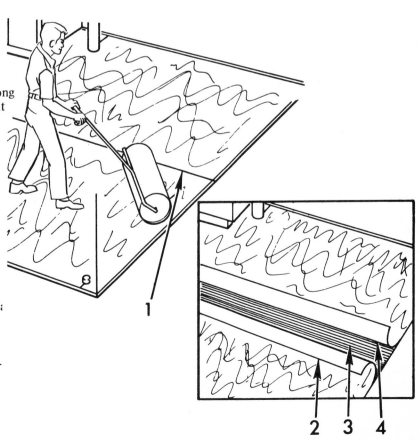

INSTALLING SHEET FLOORS

▶ **Cutting from a Pattern**

Patterns [5, 6] are used as a cutting guide in
rooms which require only one sheet and in areas
which have obstructions [1] or require irregular
cuts [2].

Patterns [5] for second and successive sheets
must be made with allowance for overlap [3].
The overlap is required for making seams.
The amount of overlap will range from a minimum of 1/4-inch for sheets with random designs
up to whatever additional amount is required by
repeated designs. Building paper or felt paper is
recommended for pattern making. However, any
sturdy material which is flexible yet not easily
torn can be used.

1. Cover area where sheet is to be installed with
    building paper. Tape sections of paper
    together to obtain required size of
    pattern [5, 6].

2. Along walls, cut pattern [5, 6] so that there
    is a 1/8-inch gap [4] between pattern and
    wall.

3. Around obstructions [1] and edges not to
    be covered by baseboards or molding, cut
    pattern [5, 6] to fit snugly with no gaps.

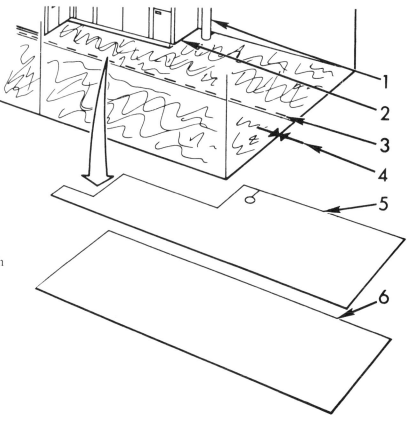

Cutting from a Pattern

4. Unroll flooring [1] with design facing up.

CAUTION

**Be sure to locate pattern [2] correctly on flooring
design. Plan position of cuts carefully to prevent
mistakes. Be sure to allow for overlap between
sheets, if required.**

5. Carefully position pattern [2] at desired
    location on flooring [1]. Secure pattern
    in place.

CAUTION

**Cutting must be done carefully and accurately,
using the pattern [2] as a guide. Make all cuts in
the same direction. Cutting stroke must be firm
enough to cut through flooring with one stroke.**

6. Using utility knife, make cutouts [3] for
    obstructions.

7. Using metal straightedge and utility knife,
    make all straight cuts.

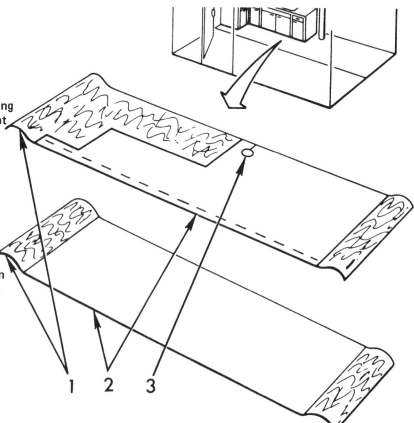

▶ **Cutting without a Pattern**

Sheet flooring should be cut without a pattern only when the area to be covered is regular in shape with no obstructions.

1. Working outside of floor area to be covered, unroll flooring [5] with design facing up.

2. Measure and record dimensions [1] of area to be covered.

CAUTION

In Step 3, flooring [5] is cut oversize to allow final trimming when at installed position.

Before performing Step 3, determine where flooring design will end at wall. If cutting second and successive sheets [3], allow for overlap [2] required to make seams. At other edges allow a minimum of 3 inches excess material [4].

3. Using straightedge and utility knife, cut flooring [5] to oversize dimensions of area to be covered.

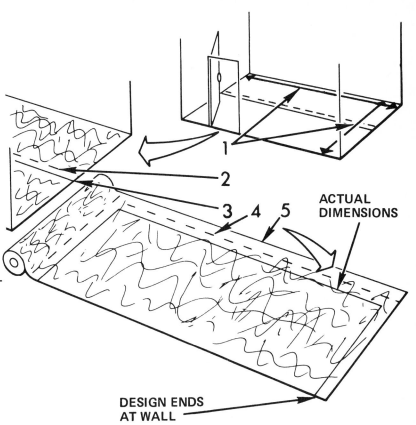

ACTUAL DIMENSIONS

DESIGN ENDS AT WALL

Cutting without a Pattern

4. Move oversize sheet [1] to installed position, allowing its edges to bend up walls.

5. Overlap sheet [1] over installed sheet [2]. Match designs with installed sheet if required.

CAUTION

Trimming must be done carefully and accurately, using a metal straightedge as a guide. Make all cuts in the same direction. Cutting strokes must be firm enough to cut through sheet [3] with one stroke.

A 1/8-inch gap [4] must be left between sheet [3] and wall after trimming to allow for expansion of the floor and walls.

6. Firmly press sheet [3] into base of wall. Using straightedge and utility knife, trim excess so that there is a 1/8-inch gap [4].

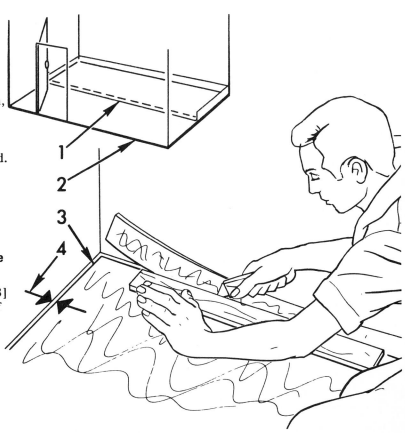

INSTALLING BASEBOARDS OR MOLDING

Either wood or vinyl baseboards and molding may be used with resilient floors.

If you plan to install vinyl cove molding [1], go to Page 34 for installation procedures.

If you plan to install wood baseboards or molding, one of the following three applications may apply to your situation:

● Install baseboard only. This application is the most common. It should be used if gap [2] between flooring and wall is narrow enough to be covered by baseboard.

● Install baseboard and shoe molding. If gap [3] between flooring and wall is too wide to be covered by baseboards alone, install shoe molding also.

● Install shoe molding only. If flooring was installed against existing baseboard [4], shoe molding must be installed to cover any gaps.

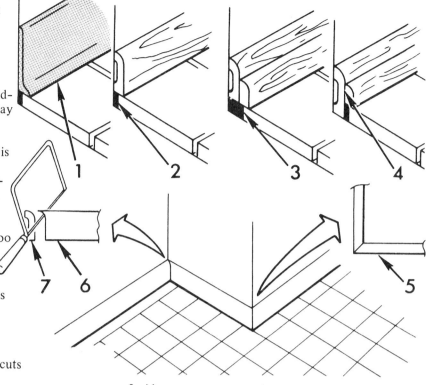

For both shoe molding and baseboards, make cuts for joints as follows:

● Outside corners – use 45 degree miter cut [5]

● Inside corners – use coping cut. Coping cut is made by cutting board [6] to fit closely against board [7].

REPAIRING RESILIENT FLOORS

▶ **Replacing Damaged Tiles**

This section describes how to replace damaged tiles installed with adhesive. Self-sticking tiles can be easily pried up and replaced.

If you do not have a matching tile, sometimes you can obtain one from another part of the floor which is not ordinarily visible. For example, you might use a tile from under the refrigerator to replace a damaged one by the entrance to the room.

The following tools and supplies are required:

Iron [1]	Aluminum foil [6]
Putty knife [2]	Paper towels
Rolling pin [3]	Tile adhesive
Notched trowel [4]	Tile

1. Cut piece of aluminum foil [6] slightly larger than old tile [5].

2. Place foil [6] over old tile [5].

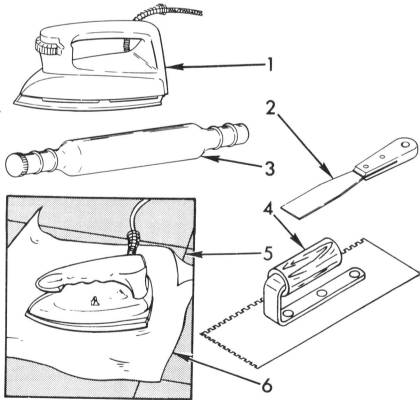

WARNING

Be careful when using hot iron to prevent burning hand or melting tile.

3. Using medium hot iron, heat foil [6] just until tile [5] is warm.

Replacing Damaged Tiles

4. Carefully insert putty knife at widest crack [1] between floor tiles.

CAUTION

Any adhesive that spreads to the face of surrounding tiles should be removed immediately before it hardens.

5. While applying heat to aluminum foil [2], push putty knife further under tile [1] until tile can be lifted and removed.

6. Place paper towel [3] over exposed adhesive [4]. Place aluminum foil [2] over paper towel.

7. Using medium hot iron, heat aluminum foil [2] until paper towel [3] is warm.

8. Remove iron. Remove foil [2]. While adhesive [4] is still warm, wipe it from floor with paper towel [3].

9. Repeat Steps 6 through 8 until no ridges of adhesive remain.

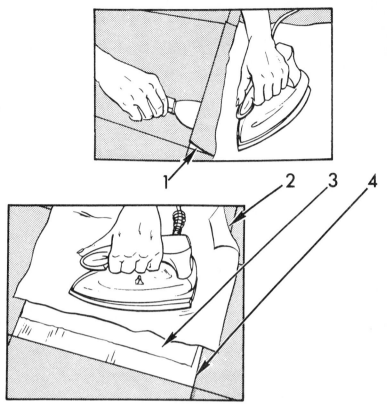

Replacing Damaged Tiles

10. Using notched trowel, apply light coat of adhesive [1] to floor.

CAUTION

When installing new tile [2], do not slide tile into place. Be sure patterns are aligned as required.

11. Carefully place new tile [2] into position.

12. Press tile [2] firmly in place.

13. Using rolling pin, apply even pressure to entire surface of new tile [2].

14. Remove excess adhesive from face of tiles with paper towel.

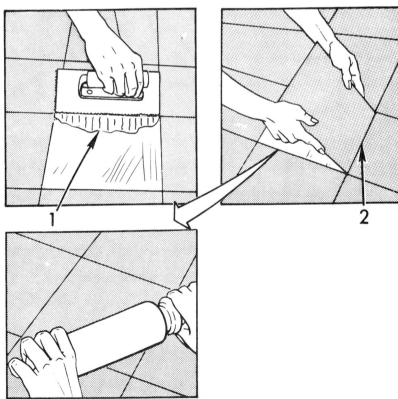

REPAIRING RESILIENT FLOORS

▶ **Replacing Damaged Sheet Flooring**

To repair sheet flooring, you will need a piece of material from original roll.

The following tools and supplies are required:

    Metal straightedge [1]
    Linoleum knife [2] or utility knife
    Iron [3]
    Putty knife [4]
    Notched trowel [5]
    Rolling pin [6]
    Aluminum foil
    Paper towels
    Tile adhesive
    Sheet flooring
    Seam sealing compound if required for your
       type of flooring

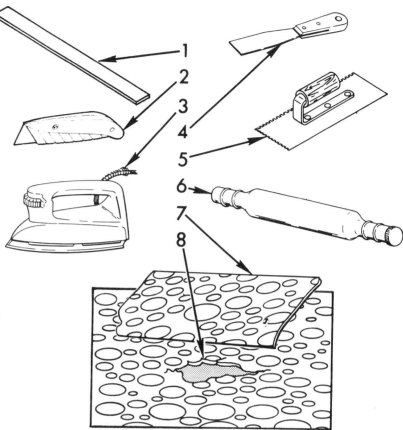

CAUTION

New piece of flooring [7] must be large enough to allow matching designs.

1. Using knife, cut new piece of flooring [7] larger than damaged area [8].

2. Place new piece of flooring [7] over damaged area [8].

3. Carefully align designs.

Replacing Damaged Sheet Flooring

CAUTION

Be sure not to move new flooring [1] when cutting.

Be sure to cut completely through new flooring [1] so that old flooring [2] is marked by knife at same time.

4. Place metal straightedge on new piece of flooring [1].

5. While firmly holding metal straightedge and new flooring [1], cut completely through new flooring with knife.

6. Remove new flooring [1].

CAUTION

Be sure not to move metal straightedge when cutting old flooring [2].

7. Place metal straightedge along newly cut lines [2].

8. Using knife and metal straightedge, cut through old flooring [2].

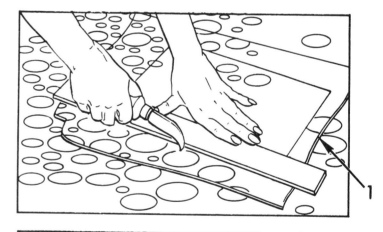

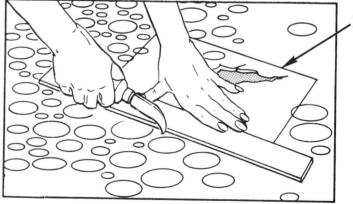

Replacing Damaged Sheet Flooring

If adhesive was not originally used to install sheet flooring, old flooring [1] can be easily lifted and removed. Go to Page 48 to install new flooring.

9. Cut piece of aluminum foil [2] slightly larger than piece of old flooring [3] to be removed.

10. Place foil over old flooring [3].

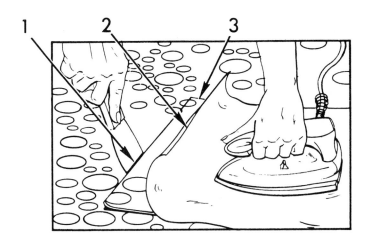

WARNING

Be careful when using hot iron to prevent burning hand or melting flooring [3].

11. Using medium hot iron, heat foil [2] just until old flooring [3] is warm.

12. Carefully insert putty knife at one cut [1] in old flooring [3].

CAUTION

Any adhesive that spreads to the face of surrounding flooring should be removed immediately before it hardens.

13. While applying heat to aluminum foil [2], push putty knife further under flooring [3] until it can be lifted and removed.

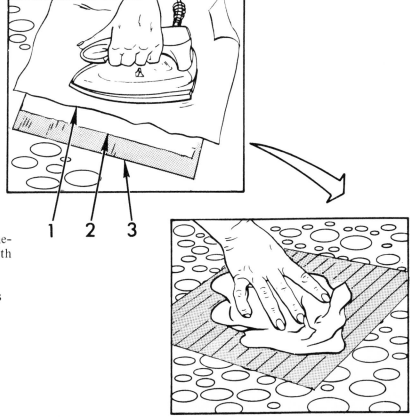

Replacing Damaged Sheet Flooring

14. Place paper towel [2] over exposed adhesive [3]. Place aluminum foil [1] over paper towel.

15. Using medium hot iron, heat aluminum foil [1] until paper towel [2] is warm.

16. Remove iron. Remove foil [1]. While adhesive [3] is still warm, wipe it from floor with paper towel [2].

17. Repeat Steps 13 through 16 until no ridges of old adhesive remain.

REPAIRING RESILIENT FLOORS

Replacing Damaged Sheet Flooring

18. Using notched trowel, apply light coat of adhesive [1] to floor.

CAUTION

When installing new flooring [2], do not slide it into place. Be sure designs are aligned as required.

19. Carefully place new piece of flooring [2] into position.

20. Press new flooring [2] firmly in place.

21. Using rolling pin, apply even pressure to entire surface of new flooring [2].

22. Remove excess adhesive from face of flooring with paper towel.

23. Apply seam sealing compound along all seams [3] if it can be used for your flooring. Follow manufacturer's instructions for its application.

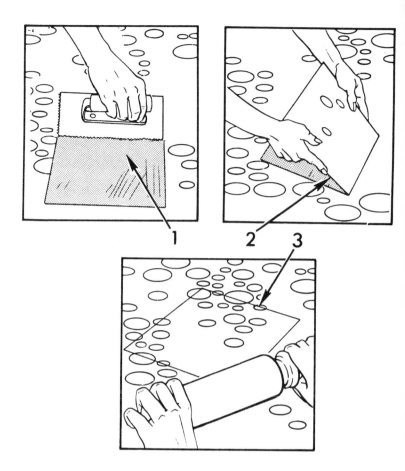

Resilient flooring goes formal or casual with equal ease.

The rich realism of hardwood parquet is superbly captured in this "Kentucky Manor" foyer floor. With an elegance that accents the stately decor, the no-wax surface is easy to maintain and resistant to stains and mildew. *Photo courtesy of Congoleum Corporation.* (left)

A distinctive Spanish motif highlights "Cedar Grove," a cushioned vinyl floor that's perfect for kitchen, living room, or den. In this all-purpose room it works for laundry, sewing, play, and living areas. *Photo courtesy of Congoleum Corporation.* (below)

Resilient flooring is always right in its favorite setting: the kitchen

The mosaic appearance of ''Castle Harbor'' has the warmth and earth-tone color needed to unify the elements of this cozy country kitchen. The easy-care vinyl flooring is cushioned for comfort and warmth underfoot. *Photo courtesy of Congoleum Corporation.* (left)

The casual charm of this kitchen is enhanced by the ''Bellaire'' vinyl floor. The pattern, available in various color combinations, realistically recreates the look of rich hand-painted tile. *Photo courtesy of Congoleum Corporation.* (below)

This unusually elegant kitchen features a no-wax sheet flooring, "Charleston Brick," designed to reproduce the look of real brick as faithfully as possible. The flooring has the "imperfections," subtle shadings of color, and variations of texture found in a real brick floor. *Photo courtesy of Armstrong Cork Company.* (top left)

The small-scale geometric tile design of "Willowbrook" cushioned vinyl flooring emphasizes the spaciousness of this pretty and functional kitchen. *Photo courtesy of Congoleum Corporation.* (top right)

Porcelain knobs, cane-bottomed chairs, and decorative molding give an old-fashioned flavor to this remodeled kitchen. Outfitted with built-in cabinets and modern appliances, the room gets added appeal from the cheerful black-and-white checkerboard floor of vinyl composition tile. *Photo courtesy of Azrock Floor Products.* (bottom right)

Flooring in a family room adapts to a variety of moods and styles.

This spacious family room, opening onto a wooded yard, is a perfect setting for ''Park Terrace,'' a fieldstone-patterned cushioned vinyl flooring. The no-wax surface is embossed for a realistic slatelike texture. *Photo courtesy of Congoleum Corporation.* (left)

Contemporary furnishings create a harmonious foil for a floor that has the timelessness of ancient Greece. ''Aegean Stone'' has the look of fragments of Grecian marble, with the design embossed on a surface composed of translucent vinyl chips containing fine particles of actual marble. Crisscross patterning of green and white feature strips ties in with the green shutters and white walls. *Photo courtesy of Azrock Floor Products.* (below left)

The modernistic Southwest Indian motif of this room is set against a complementary but unobtrusive brick-patterned flooring. ''Hampton Brick'' features inlaid color and a no-wax surface. *Photo courtesy of Armstrong Cork Company.* (below right)

52

The classic simplicity of this "Union Square" floor is an ideal backdrop for the patterned wallpaper and matching drapes. The realistic texturing and distinctive grout lines enhance this versatile cushioned vinyl design. *Photo courtesy of Congoleum Corporation.* (above)

Pretty enough for a formal setting yet practical enough for a kitchen, this "Monterrey" flooring moves graciously between the two. The random stone design gets its glossy finish from crystal-like chips embedded deep within the vinyl. *Photo courtesy of Congoleum Corporation.* (right)

Finished basements and finished attics benefit equally well from easy-care flooring.

Converting an ordinary basement to a living area is an ideal solution to a growing family. This basement was transformed by colorful wall paneling, a dropped ceiling, and a vinyl floor laid diagonally across the room in bands of contrasting colors. *Photo courtesy of Azrock Floor Products.* (left)

This once-dingy attic was remodeled back to useful life as a dormitory bedroom for teenage boys. The earth-tone colors of the vinyl floor help to conceal scuff marks, and triangles of contrasting color set apart different activity areas. *Photo courtesy of Azrock Floor Products.* (below)

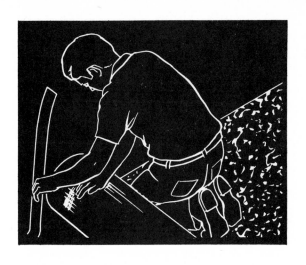

CARPETING

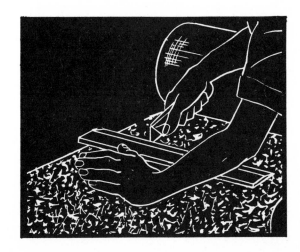

The installation of wall-to-wall carpeting has traditionally been a job for professionals. Special equipment and skills are required to do it correctly.

There is no substitute for experience and judgment if the situation presents problems such as staircases, fireplace hearths and complex room or entryway shapes.

Also, if seams are required, each situation can present unique problems. Seams should be located away from heavy traffic areas, if possible. The pieces of carpet must be matched for direction of texture and nap as well as for any design pattern. The cutting of pieces must be accomplished precisely so that there are no gaps. Finally, the pieces must be attached securely to each other so that there is no danger that they will separate under wear and tear.

Wall-to-wall carpeting represents a considerable investment. The cost of installation by professionals is modest relative to the cost of the carpet and padding. Mistakes in installation can be costly and many situations provide opportunities for making mistakes. Therefore, it is recommended that the installation of good quality wall-to-wall carpeting be done by professionals.

Fortunately for the home pro who wishes to do his own carpet installation, manufacturers are now making carpeting designed especially for easy installation. These carpets require no padding and no stretching and tacking. Also, the making of seams is simplified. No special tools are needed to install this carpeting. With care, the home pro can achieve good results.

Easy-installation carpeting is available in a large variety of textures, colors, designs and materials. These materials are being continually improved with regard to such qualities as durability, color fastness, resistance to soiling and textures. Textures range from plushes to heavy shags. With the coarser textures, it is easy to conceal gaps and seams.

Two types of carpeting are available:

● Cushion-backed (or foam padded)
● Indoor-outdoor

Cushion-backed carpets are used indoors. The foam padding is built into the carpet. It cushions the carpet to provide a soft feel underfoot. Textures range from plush to long shag.

Indoor-outdoor carpets are especially designed to resist soiling and to promote easy cleaning. For these reasons, they are often used in kitchens and game-rooms.

The chart describes the types of easy-installation carpeting presently available.

	Tiles[1]	Strips[2]	Rolls[3]
Cushion-Backed	X	X	X
Indoor-Outdoor			X

1. Tiles. Available in squares: 12 in. x 12 in. and 18 in. x 18 in. They are provided with self-sticking backing. For installation procedures, go to Page 58.

2. Strips. Available in sheets 3 ft x 5 ft. They are provided with self-sticking backing. For installation procedures, go to Page 58.

3. Rolls. Commonly range from 3 ft to 12 ft in width. Some manufacturers produce 15 ft widths. Rolls are available in any length.

   To reduce the number of seams required, order the widest carpeting suitable for your situation.

   These carpets do not have self-sticking backing. However, they lay well and in some cases no adhesive is required to hold them in place. If adhesive is required, double-face tape is commonly used. Adhesive is also available in aerosol cans for convenient application at edges of carpeting. For installation procedures, go to Page 62.

In most cases, very little preparation is required for installing carpeting. It is best to first remove all furniture from the room to provide as much open working space as possible. Then remove shoe molding, if installed, and check and repair the floor surfaces.

▶ Removing Shoe Molding

Shoe molding [2] is a rounded strip of molding which is installed between the baseboard [1] and floor. It is found in many homes.

Shoe molding [2] is fastened to the baseboard [1] with finishing nails [4]. It must be removed before you install carpeting.

Shoe molding [2] is often installed over carpeting in order to cover gaps between the carpet and the baseboard. It also helps hold the carpet in place along the wall. If you work carefully in removing it, you may be able to salvage it for re-use later.

Work carefully to avoid damaging baseboard [1] or shoe molding [2].

1.   Using sharp knife, cut paint seal along joint [3].

2.   Using block of wood and screwdriver or putty knife, carefully pry shoe molding [2] from baseboard [1].

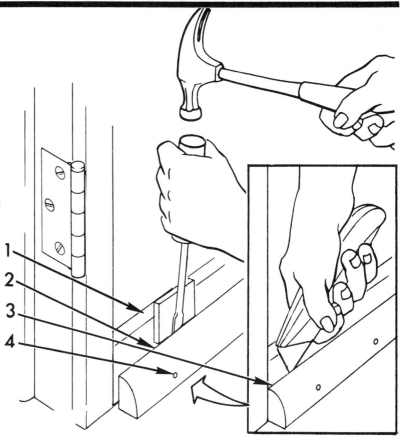

▶ Checking Floor Surfaces

Cushion-backed and indoor-outdoor carpets may be installed on the following surfaces:

● Wood

● Concrete

● Resilient

Because carpet will flex slightly with floor movement the subfloor does not have to be as rigid as with some floor coverings.

However, the floor must be fairly rigid or the carpet may pull from its tape. The seams may then split if they run parallel with floor boards.

The subfloor must be extremely dry. A slightly damp subfloor may cause mildew or even cause carpet rot. Also, tape will not adhere to a damp floor.

Before beginning to install carpets, carefully check the floor and make any necessary repairs.

▶ Checking a Wood Floor

A wood floor must be firm, even and clean before carpets can be installed.

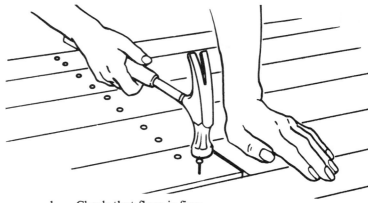

1.   Check that floor is firm.

2.   Check floor for the following problems:

● Nails protruding from floor

● Loose boards

● High or low spots

● Cracks or gaps

If any problems are found, they must be repaired.

A commercial wax remover should be used to remove all old wax from floor.

3.   Remove all old wax from floor.

PREPARATION FOR CARPETING

▶ Checking a Concrete Floor

A concrete floor must be level, clean and sealed before carpets can be installed.

1. Check floor for the following problems:
    *   High or low spots
    *   Cracks or gaps
    *   Moisture

If any problems are found, they must be repaired.

2. Clean floor surface to remove all oil, dirt or grease.

Floor surface must be sealed to give a proper surface for the tape to adhere. Ask a paint dealer what sealer should be used.

3. Seal floor.

▶ Checking a Resilient Floor

A resilient floor must be even and clean before carpets can be installed.

1. Check floor for the following problems:

    *   Loose tiles

    *   Chipped or cracked tiles
    *   Cracks or gaps on surface

If any problems are found, they must be repaired.

A commercial wax remover should be used to remove all old wax from floor.

2. Remove all old wax from floor.

▬ INSTALLING TILE OR STRIP CARPETING ▬

▼ Planning and Estimating

Plan the job carefully so that you start the job with everything you need to complete it.

1. Measure and record all floor dimensions. Include door openings [1] and obstructions.

2. Letting each square equal 1 foot, draw floor plan on graph paper.

If you are planning to use carpet tiles which have designs, the completed floor will look best if opposite borders are symmetrical. This means that the width of border A should be the same as the width of border C; the width of border B should be the same as the width of border D.

If you are planning to use tiles or strips which do not have designs (for example, shag textures), it is not necessary that the borders be symmetrical.

3. Make layout of tiles or strips on floor plan. Adjust layout until borders are symmetrical, if required.

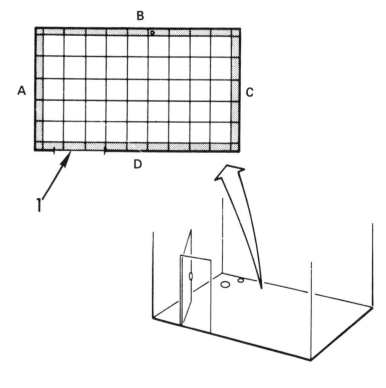

Planning and Estimating

All border tiles or strips should be made wide enough that they will stick well to the floor. Allow a minimum width of 4 inches.

4. Check layout [1] to determine that all borders are at least 4 inches wide.

If borders do not need to be symmetrical, adjust layout by moving it up or down and right or left, as required [2].

If borders are planned to be symmetrical, adjust layout by moving it one-half tile width (or length) up or down and right or left, as required [3].

5. Determine number of tiles or strips required from layout.

It may be difficult to find matching carpeting in the future. Therefore, it is a good idea to obtain 1 or 2 extra tiles or strips for future repairs.

6. Determine amounts of shoe molding, if desired, from perimeter dimensions of room.

Binder bars must be used at doorways to protect carpeting if edges are exposed. See section below.

7. Determine number and lengths of binder bars required from layout.

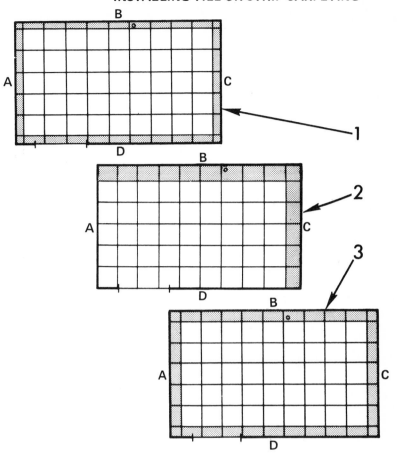

▶ Tools and Supplies

The following tools and supplies are required to install tile or strip carpeting:

> Utility knife [1] for cutting carpet.
> Metal straightedge [2] for guiding the knife.
> Hammer [3] or screwdriver [4] for installing binder bar.
> Tape measure [5] for squaring off floor.
> Chalk line [6] for squaring off floor.
> Binder bar [7] for protecting and holding down edges of carpet at doorway if carpeting ends at doorway — i.e., floor surface changes to tile, wood, etc.
> Carpet

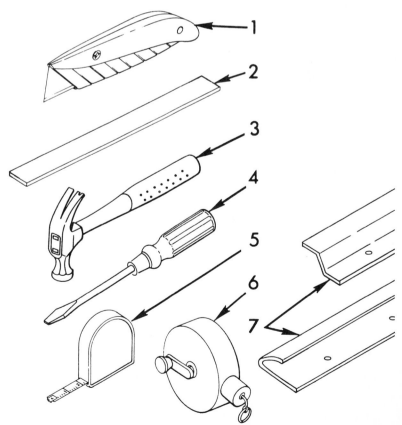

INSTALLING TILE OR STRIP CARPETING

▶ **Selecting a Starting Place**

It is easiest to begin carpet laying along an unobstructed wall. Preferably, the wall should be a dominant or most frequently seen wall.

It is usually most convenient to start at a corner opposite a doorway [2]. However, be sure that you start at a corner which is square (90 degrees).

To determine whether a corner is square, perform the following Steps:

1. Measure 4 feet from corner [1] and place mark [3] on floor as close as possible to wall.

2. Measure 3 feet from corner [1] and place mark [4] on floor as close as possible to wall.

Distance between marks [3, 4] will be 5 feet if corner [1] is square.

3. Check that distance between marks is 5 feet.

If distance is 5 feet, corner is square. Go to section below.

If distance is not 5 feet, corner is not square. Check and select another corner.

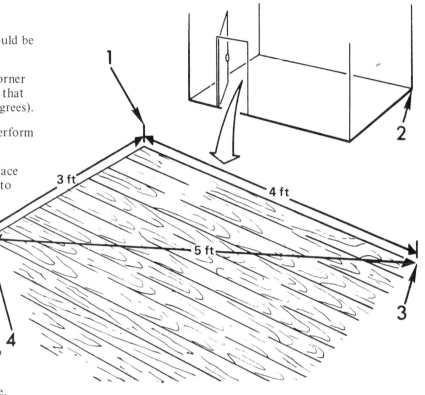

Selecting a Starting Place

If tiles or strips in borders are whole pieces, floor does not need to be marked for laying carpet. Go to Page 61.

If tiles or strips in borders are less than whole pieces, floor must be marked. Go to Step 4.

4. From drawing of floor, determine width of border along one wall adjoining square corner.

5. Place marks [1,3] on floor at distance from wall determined in Step 4.

6. Using chalk line, make a straight line [2] between marks [1,3].

7. From drawing of floor, determine width of border along other wall adjoining square corner.

8. Place marks [4,6] on floor at distance from wall determined in Step 7.

9. Using chalk line, make a straight line [5] between marks [4,6].

The two lines [2,5] are used for aligning the tiles or strips. See Page 61, Sequence B.

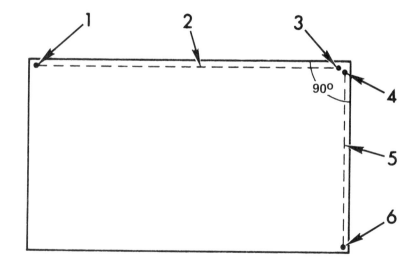

▶ **Cutting Carpeting**

Carpeting is easily cut with a sharp utility knife. For heavy textured carpets (shags), it is some-times easier to cut if piece is turned over and cut is made from underside.

▶ **Cutting Straight Edges**

1. Position and hold straightedge firmly against carpet at line to be cut. If you have shag carpet, first separate shag along line to be cut to expose backing.

2. Using sharp utility knife, cut along straight-edge [1] with firm stroke.

▶ **Cutting around Obstructions**

1. Mark location of obstruction on carpet.

2. Holding straightedge firmly on carpet, make slit [2] from edge of carpet to location of obstruction.

3. Position and hold carpet firmly against obstruction [3].

4. Cut closely around obstruction. There should be no gap between carpet and obstruction.

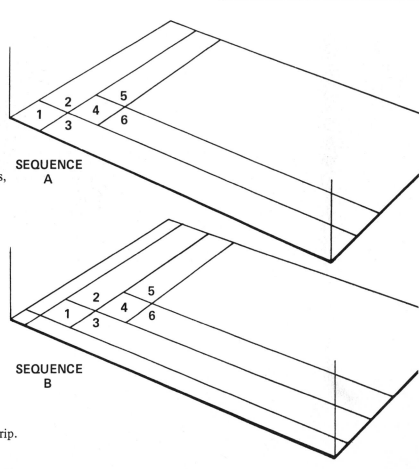

▶ **Laying Tiles or Strips**

Before beginning to lay carpet, read through

● Preparation for Carpeting, Page 57.
● Selecting a Starting Place, Page 60.
● Cutting Carpeting, above.

If whole tiles or strips are being used in borders, install them in accordance with Sequence A.

● Install corner tile 1; install rows 2 and 3.
● Install corner tile 4; install rows 5 and 6. Continue sequence.

If part tiles or strips are being used in borders, install them in accordance with Sequence B.

● Install corner tile 1; install rows 2 and 3.
● Install corner tile 4; install rows 5 and 6. Continue sequence until all whole tiles are installed.
● Install all border tiles. Measure, cut and trim to fit one at a time.

1. Remove protective backing from tile or strip.

INSTALLING TILE OR STRIP CARPETING

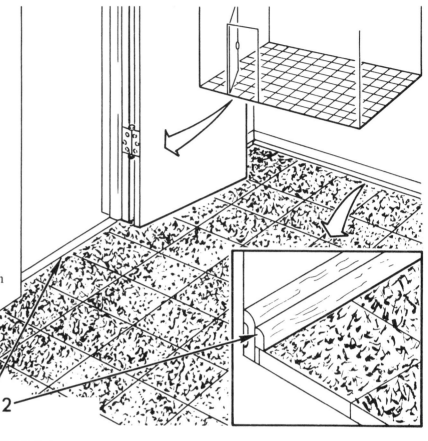

Laying Tiles or Strips

2. Position tile or strip on floor.

3. Press firmly over entire surface of tile or strip to secure to floor.

4. Install shoe molding [2] if desired. Page 70.

5. Install binder bars [1] in accordance with manufacturer's instructions.

▬ INSTALLING ROLL CARPETING ▬

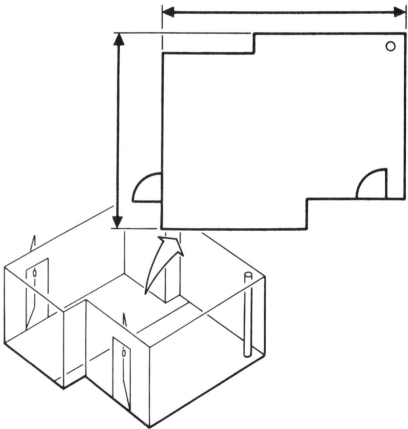

▶ Planning and Estimating

To estimate the amount of materials needed, you should make a detailed sketch of the floor to be covered. Graph paper is very handy for making this sketch.

Measure and record all dimensions on the sketch. Be sure to include door openings and obstructions.

Take the sketch to a dealer. He will help you determine:

● The best width of carpet to buy to keep the number of seams at a minimum and to minimize the amount of waste carpeting.

● The best locations for any seams which are required.

● The kinds and amounts of installation materials required such as double-face tape, seam tape, and, at doorways, binder bars.

To estimate materials yourself, see Page 68.

Planning and Estimating

Estimate materials as follows:

Carpet. Determine number of square feet of coverage required from sketch. As a general rule, select carpet widths which will eliminate seams, if possible. If you cannot avoid seams, locate them away from heavy traffic areas.

Seam tape [1]. Determine total length of all seams from sketch to estimate length of seam tape required.

Double-face tape [2]. Double-face tape is used to secure carpet at all edges around room and obstructions. At doorways, additional strips are required. Also, if room is longer than 20 feet, apply double-face tape across floor at 10 foot intervals or less.

Binder bars. Binder bars are used at doorways to protect exposed edges of carpet. Determine number and length of binder bars from sketch.

Molding. Determine length of molding required from perimeter dimensions of room. Some installers prefer to use shoe molding to help hold down edges of carpet.

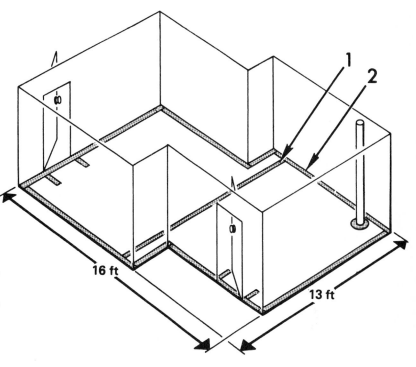

16 ft

13 ft

▶ **Tools and Supplies**

The following tools and supplies are required to install roll carpeting:

    Utility knife [1] for cutting carpeting
    Metal straightedge [2] for guiding the knife
    Scissors [3] for cutting tape
    Chalk line [4] for marking carpet when
       making seams
    Hammer [5] or screwdriver [6] for install-
       ing binder bar
    Binder bar [7] for protecting and holding
       down edges of carpet at doorway if carpet-
       ing ends at doorway — i.e., floor surface
       changes to tile, wood, etc.
    Carpet
    Double-face tape
    Seaming tape, if required

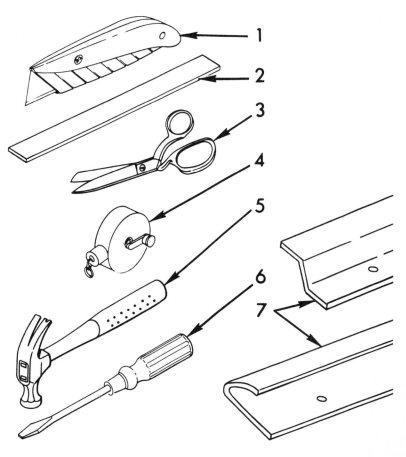

INSTALLING ROLL CARPETING

▶ **Cutting Carpeting**

These procedures describe how to cut carpets.
Do not cut carpets until you have read entirely
through:

● Making Seams, Page 65.
● Laying Rolls, Page 68.

Carpeting is easily cut with a sharp utility knife.
For heavy textured carpets (shags), it is sometimes easier to cut if piece is turned over and cut
is made from underside.

▶ **Cutting Straight Edges**

Piece of carpet must be cut oversize before
positioning it in room. Final fitting and cutting
is then completed after piece is located in its
installed position.

1. Using chalk, mark lines [1] to be cut on
    carpet. Allow 2 inches or more extra length
    at all edges to be fitted. Be sure that designs
    and direction of material nap match
    previously fitted pieces.

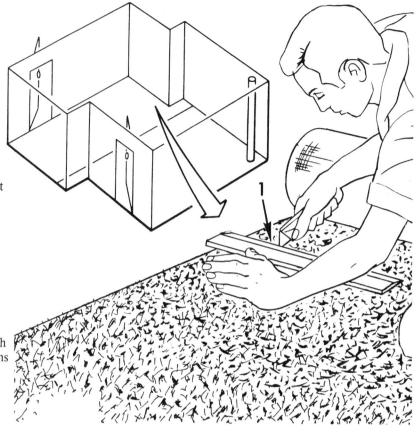

Cutting Straight Edges

2. Position and hold straightedge [3] firmly
    against carpet on line to be cut. If you have
    shag carpet, first separate shag along line to
    be cut to expose backing.

3. Using sharp utility knife, cut along straight-
    edge [3] with firm stroke.

4. Place carpet in installed position. Be sure
    that designs and nap are matched with pre-
    viously installed pieces, if required.

When cutting extra carpet [2] from edge, be sure
that carpet is pressed tightly into corner [1]
where floor and wall meet.

5. Press carpet firmly into corner [1].

6. Using sharp utility knife, cut carpet at
    corner [1].

7. Fit and cut remaining edges, as required.

After carpet is cut to fit, check fit at all edges.
Trim carpet as required.

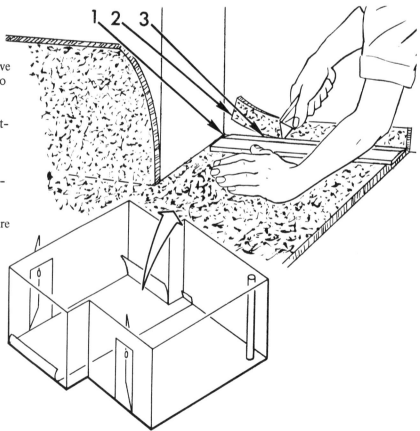

▶ **Cutting Around Obstructions**

1. Mark location of obstruction [1] on carpet.

2. Holding straightedge firmly on carpet, make slit [2] from edge of carpet to location of obstruction.

3. Position and hold carpet firmly against obstruction [1].

4. Cut closely around obstruction [1]. There should be no gap between carpet and obstruction.

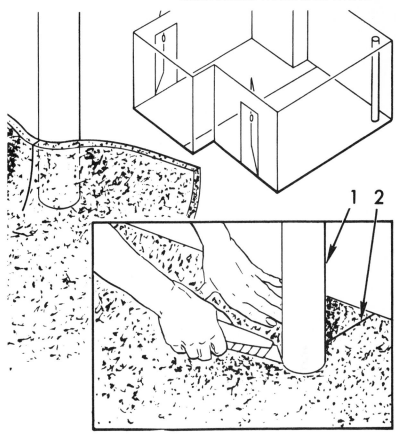

▶ **Making Seams**

First piece [1] of carpet must be at installed position. It has been cut and trimmed to fit. It has not been secured to floor.

When placing second piece [2] of carpet in position, be sure that designs, if any, are matched with first piece [1]. Also, be sure that direction of nap runs in same direction, if required.

If carpet does not have a design, extra length [3] at edges should be about 2 inches.

If carpet has a design, extra length may vary after designs are matched.

1. Place second piece [2] of carpet tightly against first piece [1].

2. Align designs, if required.

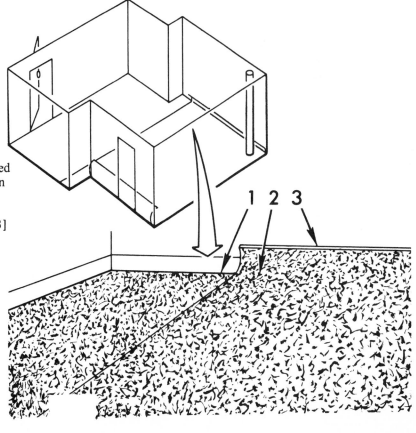

INSTALLING ROLL CARPETING

Making Seams

Be sure that designs stay aligned when smoothing second piece [2] of carpet. Be sure that carpet is flat, smooth and touching first piece [1] of carpet.

4. Using utility knife, trim extra length from ends of piece [2].

Marks [3] should be made on both carpets at seam. These marks are a guide for keeping the carpets aligned.

5. Using chalk, make several marks [3] at seam.

6. Push second piece [2] of carpet against first piece [1] of carpet to form a slight peak at the seam [4].

7. Check that there are no gaps between the two sections of carpet along the entire length of the seam [4].

If gaps are not found, go to Step 8.

If gaps are found, the carpet must be cut to make a better fit. Go to Page 67 for procedures for making a double cut.

Making Seams

8. Pull second piece [4] of carpet away from first piece [1].

A line [3] must be placed on floor as a guide for laying the seam tape [2]. The edge of the first piece [1] of carpet should be used as a guide for making the line.

9. Using pencil or chalk, draw a line [3] on the floor the entire length of the carpet.

When placing seam tape [2] on the line be sure that non-adhesive side is against the floor and the adhesive side is facing up.

The edge of the first piece [1] of carpet must be lifted slightly and held away from floor.

Tape [2] must be applied along the entire length of the line [3]. Tape must be centered over the line.

10. Place seam tape [2] on line [3].

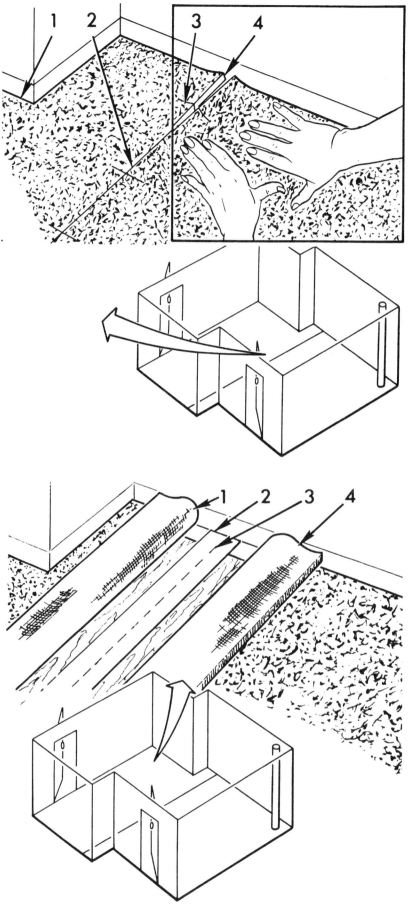

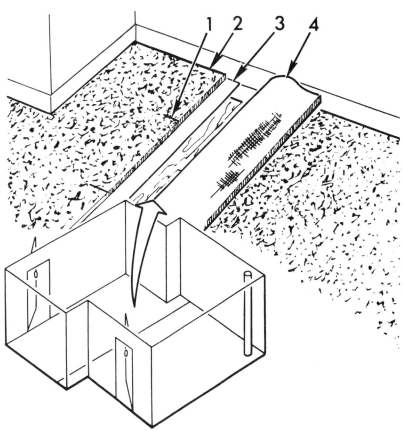

Making Seams

11. Place edge of first piece [2] of carpet on tape [3]. Edge will come to center of tape.

12. Pull edge of second piece [4] of carpet slightly over edge of first piece [2]. Align chalk marks [1].

When pulling second piece [4], pull slowly so that its edge just drops from edge of first piece [2] onto the tape, to make a tight seam. If carpet has a long shag, be careful not to pull shag onto tape.

13. Slowly pull second piece [4] until edge drops onto tape [3].

14. Press down edges of both strips [2, 4] to make a smooth seam.

Repeat Steps 1 through 14 for making seams in any remaining pieces of carpet.

Making a Double Cut

Edges between pieces of carpet may not fit together well. This condition is particularly likely when you are piecing together remnants to reduce waste. A tight fitting seam can be made easily by double cutting the pieces.

The pieces of carpet are aligned by overlapping the two adjoining edges and cutting through both at the same time.

If the carpet has a repeated design, the pieces must be overlapped so that the designs match. After you have matched the designs, locate a straightedge on the overlap as required to make a straight seam. Go to Step 6 to cut seam.

If the carpet does not have a repeated design, you may use a minimum overlap. Go to Step 1.

1. Place marks [2, 6] 1 inch from edge [3] of first piece [1] of carpet.

2. Secure chalk line at one mark. Pull chalk line to other mark.

3. Hold chalk line tight. Pull chalk line straight up from carpet. Release chalk line.

Chalk line will leave a straight line [7] on the carpet.

4. Repeat Steps 1 through 3 on second piece [4] of carpet. Mark edge [5] which adjoins first piece [1].

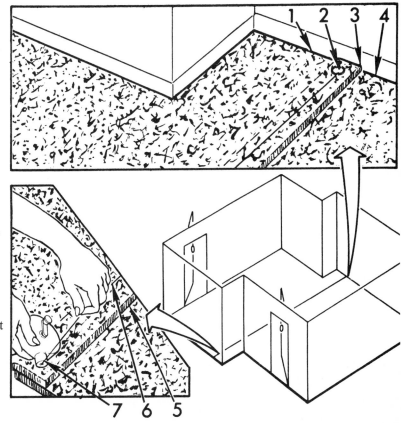

INSTALLING ROLL CARPETING

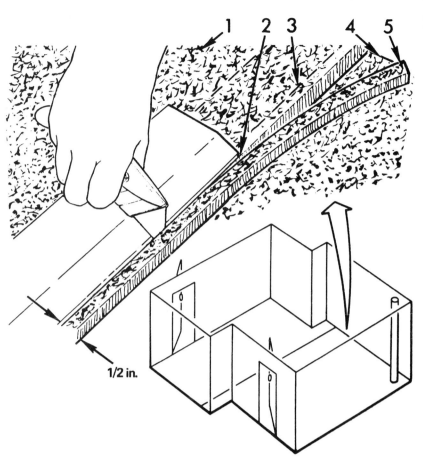

Making a Double Cut

5.   Place edge of one piece [1] over edge of other piece [4]. Align edge of top piece with chalk line on bottom piece.

Cut [2] should be made 1/2-inch from edge of top carpet.

Be sure to hold utility knife vertically when making cut.

6.   Using straightedge and utility knife, cut through both pieces [1, 4].

7.   Remove strip [5] from top piece [1]. Lift top piece. Remove strip [3] from bottom piece [4].

8.   Go to Page 66, Step 8 to complete making seam.

1/2 in.

▶ **Laying Rolls**

Before beginning to lay rolls, read through:

●   Preparation for Carpeting, Page 57.
●   Cutting Carpeting, Page 61.
●   Making Seams, Page 65.

1.   Cut all pieces to exact size.

2.   Make all seams so that carpet is in one piece.

When applying double-face tape to floor, stick tape only to floor. Be sure not to remove protective paper from top of tape.

3.   Apply tape [1] to floor as shown:

●   Along all edges around room
●   Around obstructions
●   At both sides and fronts of doorways
●   At approximate 10-foot intervals in rooms exceeding 20 feet in length.

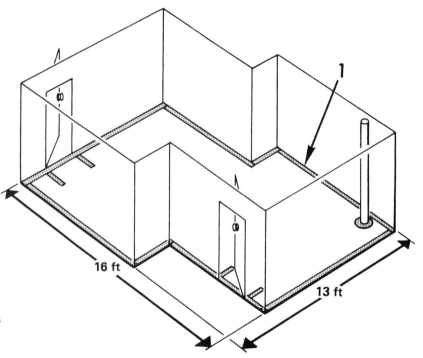

16 ft

13 ft

68

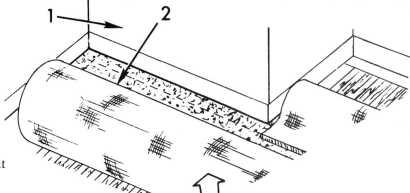

Laying Rolls

4. Lay out carpet [2] on floor and check that it fits room.

5. Roll carpet [2] up and position it at starting wall [1].

6. Remove protective paper from tape along wall [1].

7. Unroll end of carpet. Press carpet into tape.

Laying Rolls

Carpet must be pulled tightly as it is unrolled to prevent wrinkles, bulges or air pockets.

One person working at each side wall makes installation easier and permits the carpet to be pulled tighter as it is being unrolled.

Remove protective paper from tape as you come to it.

8. Unroll carpet [1] along side wall [2]. Press carpet firmly into tape.

9. Align carpet [1] with end wall. Press firmly into tape.

10. Install shoe molding, if required. Page 70.

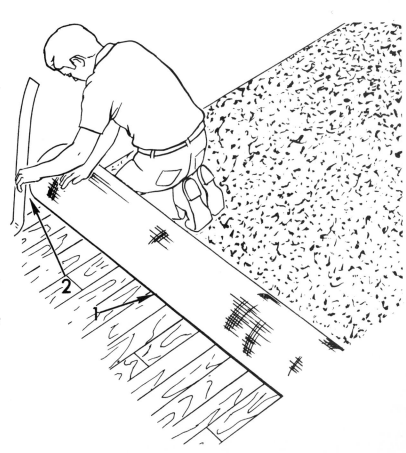

69

INSTALLING BASEBOARDS OR MOLDING

Either wood or vinyl baseboards and molding may be used with carpeting. However, if walls are paneled with wood and carpeting extends from wall-to-wall, baseboards and molding are sometimes omitted entirely.

If you plan to install vinyl cove molding [1], see Page 34 for installation procedures.

If you plan to install shoe molding [2], continue.

Shoe molding [2] is used to cover gaps [3] between the carpet and baseboards. It is also used to help secure the edges of the carpet to the floor. When installing shoe molding, hold it firmly against carpet.

Shoe molding is fastened to baseboards with finishing nails. It is a good idea to paint or stain the molding before installing it to avoid soiling the carpet.

Make corner joints for shoe molding as follows:

- Outside corners – use 45 degree miter cut [4]
- Inside corners – use coping cut. Coping cut is made by cutting board [5] to fit closely against board [6].

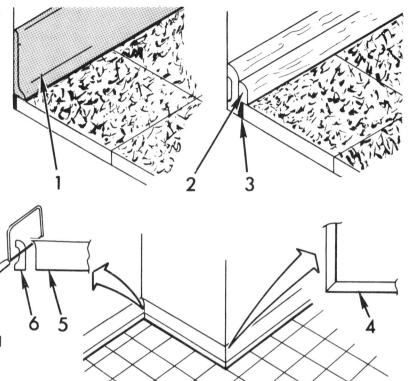

REPAIRING CARPETS

▶ **Repairing Large Damaged Areas in Cushion-Backed and Indoor-Outdoor Carpets**

Repairing a damaged area in cushion-backed carpet or indoor-outdoor carpets consists of cutting the damaged area from the carpet and installing a new section of carpet.

If carpet tiles are installed, they are not repaired. A damaged tile is removed and a new tile is installed.

If spare carpet is not available for making the repair, remove carpeting from a closet to obtain a piece to make the repair.

The following tools and supplies are required:

    Utility knife [1]
    Double-face tape

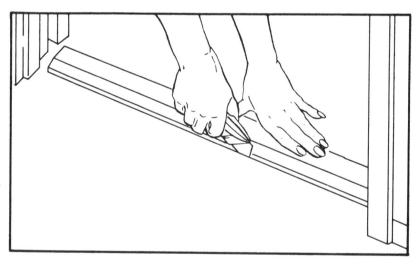

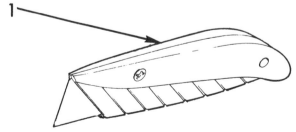

Repairing Large Damaged Areas in Cushion-Backed and Indoor-Outdoor Carpets

When cutting damaged area [1] from carpet, try to make cut between rows of pile.

When cutting the damaged area [1], cut should be made in a square [2] shape.

1. Using utility knife, cut damaged area [1] from carpet.

A patch must be cut the same size as the piece removed from the floor. The cut piece should be used as a guide to make sure the patch is the correct size.

If the carpet has a repeated design, be sure to match designs before cutting.

2. Using utility knife, cut replacement patch.

Floor must be completely cleaned or tape will not adhere to the floor. The exposed floor and approximately 3 inches of floor beneath the carpet must be cleaned.

3. Clean the surface.

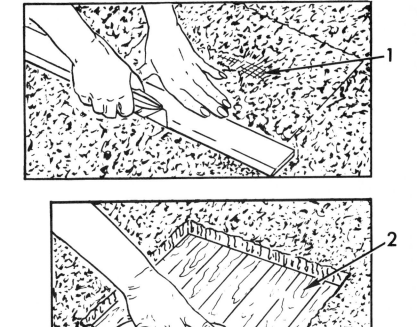

Repairing Large Damaged Areas in Cushion-Backed and Indoor-Outdoor Carpets

Double-faced tape [1] is used to secure the patch to the surrounding carpet. The tape must be cut so it will not overlap when placed under the carpet.

The tape may be cut with miter edges [2] or square edges [3].

4. Measure and cut four pieces of tape [1].

When applying double-face tape to floor, stick tape only to floor. Be sure not to remove protective paper from top of tape.

Approximately one-half the width of the tape [1] is placed under the edges of the installed carpet with adhesive side against the floor.

Install one piece of tape at a time.

5. Lift edge of carpet. Place tape [1] under carpet.

6. Repeat Step 5 for remaining edges.

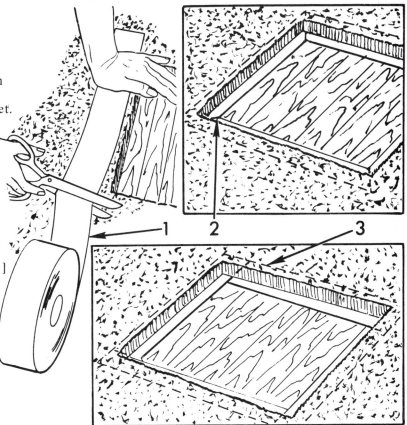

Repairing Large Damaged Areas in Cushion-Backed and Indoor-Outdoor Carpets

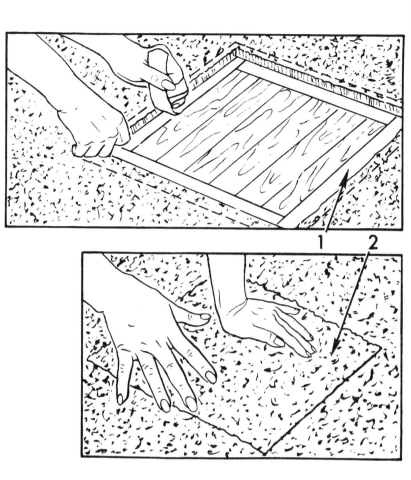

7.   While lifting all four edges of carpet, remove protecting paper from all tape [1].

8.   Lower carpet onto tape [1]. Press firmly into tape.

9.   Place patch [2] in opening. Press firmly on all four edges.

10. Press and smooth center of patch until patch is level with surrounding carpet.

Pile can be blended by forcing pile together with your fingers.

11. Blend pile together around seams.

▶ **Repairing Tears in Cushion-Backed or Indoor-Outdoor Carpets**

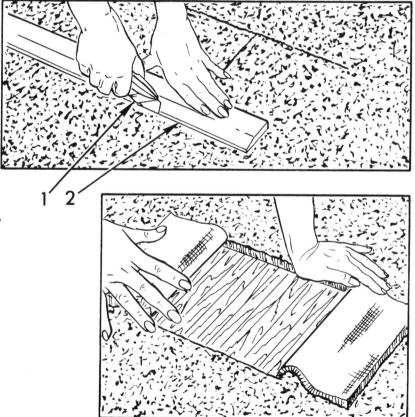

Repairing a tear in cushion-backed carpet or indoor-outdoor carpet consists of cutting the carpet around the tear and folding it away from the floor. Then tape the carpet to the floor.

When tears or other damage occur to carpet tiles, it is easier to replace the tile than to repair it.

The following tools and supplies are required:

    Utility knife [1]
    Metal straightedge [2]
    Double-face tape

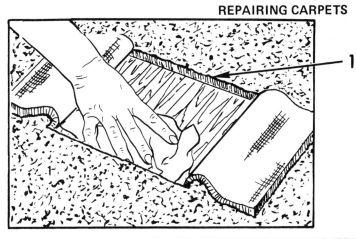

Repairing Tears in Cushion-Backed or Indoor-Outdoor Carpets

When cutting two perpendicular cuts [1], try to make cuts between rows of pile. The cuts must be long enough to allow the carpet to be folded and tape applied underneath. The cuts must be made completely through the carpet. Cuts must be made at each end of tear.

1. Using utility knife and straightedge, make a cut [1] at each end of tear. Fold back two flaps made by the cuts.

Floor must be completely clean or tape will not adhere to the floor. The exposed floor and approximately 3 inches of floor beneath the carpet must be cleaned.

2. Clean floor surface.

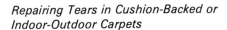

Repairing Tears in Cushion-Backed or Indoor-Outdoor Carpets

Double-faced tape [2] is used to secure the edges [1] of the surrounding carpet to the floor. The tape must be cut so it will not overlap when placed under the carpet.

3. Measure and cut four pieces of tape [2].

The whole width of the tape [2] must be placed under the edges [1] of the surrounding carpet with adhesive side against the floor.

4. Carefully lift edge [1] of surrounding carpet. Place tape [2] under edge. Press tape firmly against floor.

5. Repeat Step 4 for three remaining edges [1].

6. While lifting edges [1] from floor, remove protective paper from tape [2]. Place edges against tape. Press firmly into tape.

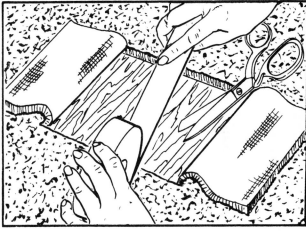

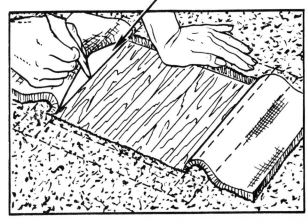

REPAIRING CARPETS

Repairing Tears in Cushion-Backed or Indoor-Outdoor Carpets

Double-faced tape [3] is used to secure the two flaps [1] to the floor. The tape must be cut so it will not overlap when placed on the flaps.

The tape may be cut with miter edges [4] or square edges [2].

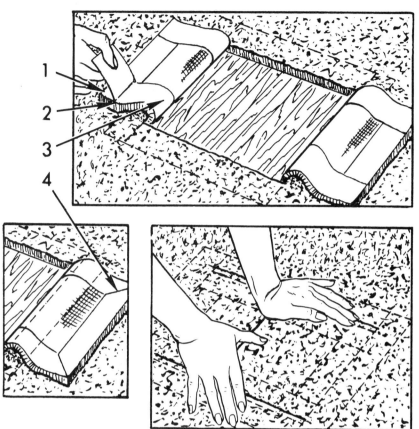

7. Measure and cut three pieces of tape [3] for each flap [1].

The tape [3] must be applied to the three edges of each flap [1] with adhesive side against the flaps.

8. Apply three pieces of tape [3] to each flap [1].

9. Remove protective paper from tape [3] on one flap [1]. Fold flap against the floor. Press firmly against floor.

10. Repeat Step 9 for other flap.

Pile can be blended by forcing the pile together with your fingers.

11. Blend pile together around all seams.

The luxury of carpeting pulls together any decorating scheme.

The Oriental richness of the upholstery fabric in this comfortable living room is effectively offset by the sleek simplicity of "Amour" carpeting and the chrome-and-glass accent pieces. *Photo courtesy of Bigelow-Sanford, Inc., A Sperry and Hutchinson Company.* (above)

The textured "Carmel" carpeting is a handsome complement to the floral-print sofas and elaborate moldings of this elegant but cozy room. *Photo courtesy of Milliken Carpets.* (right)

Carpeting styles are as diverse as the rooms they decorate.

"Promenade" carpeting provides a smooth backdrop for the busy look created by the shutters and the fabric pattern. *Photo courtesy of Bigelow-Sanford, Inc., A Sperry and Hutchinson Company.* (above left)

The light Oriental motif of this living room is enriched by the "Celestra" carpeting underfoot. *Photo courtesy of Milliken Carpets.* (above right)

The serene stateliness of this wood-paneled room is beautifully underscored by the muted elegance of the "Chamade" carpeting. *Photo courtesy of Bigelow-Sanford, Inc., A Sperry and Hutchinson Company.* (left)

Natural-weave and pale velour upholstery are a perfect foil for the modernistic pattern of "Beauvais" carpeting. *Photo courtesy of Bigelow-Sanford, Inc., A Sperry and Hutchinson Company.* (facing page, top)

The stripes in this unusual carpet separate the apartment's entrance foyer from its living area. Window Covering: Flexalum Decor Blinds by Hunter Douglas, Inc. *Photo courtesy of Hunter Douglas Window Products Division.* (facing page, bottom left)

The unusual textured patterning of the "Tiffany Touch" carpet adds interest to this correspondence corner. *Photo courtesy of World Carpets.* (facing page, bottom right)

Carpeting adds a new dimension to dining elegance.

A rich floral-print upholstery, a roaring fire, and "Candescence" carpeting make this living/dining area a warm and gracious spot for relaxing or entertaining. *Photo courtesy of Bigelow-Sanford, Inc., A Sperry and Hutchinson Company.* (facing page, top)

The elegant formality of this dining room is perfectly underscored by the velvety richness of "Inheritance" carpeting. Furniture: American Drew, A Sperry and Hutchinson Company. *Photo courtesy of Bigelow-Sanford, Inc., A Sperry and Hutchinson Company.* (facing page, bottom)

The subtle floral pattern of "Formal Elegance" carpeting adds visual interest to the elegant austerity of this formal setting. *Photo courtesy of Milliken Carpets.* (right)

Lushly textured "Monterey" carpeting is an effective contrast to the sleek simplicity of this contemporary dining group. *Photo courtesy of Bigelow-Sanford, Inc., A Sperry and Hutchinson Company.* (below)

The warmth of carpeting makes it a natural for bedrooms.

The rich formality of this Old World bedroom is accentuated by the "Katsura" carpeting, which covers the wall behind the bed as well as the floor. Furniture: "Chaumont" by American Drew, A Sperry and Hutchinson Company. *Photo courtesy of Bigelow-Sanford, Inc., A Sperry and Hutchinson Company.* (left)

This gaily decorated room, suited to sleeping or working, features a cheerful orange carpet. *Photo courtesy of World Carpets.* (below left)

The combination of Colonial-print wallpaper, quilted comforter, and "Endearment" carpeting creates the cozy warmth of this old-fashioned room. *Photo courtesy of Bigelow-Sanford, Inc., A Sperry and Hutchinson Company.* (below right)

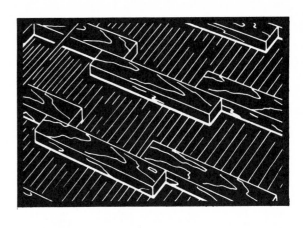

WOOD FLOORS

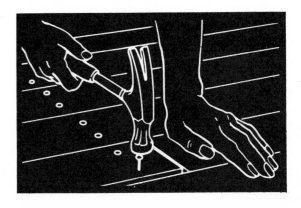

Wood floors are some of the most beautiful and durable floors available. Because no two pieces of wood are alike, every wood floor is unique.

With minimum maintenance, a wood floor will usually last the life of any home. Modern products now make the maintenance of wood floors easier than ever before. With today's finishes and waxes, a floor will last for many years before refinishing is required.

There are generally two types of wood floors available: Hardwood floors and block or parquet floors.

Hardwood floors, made of long boards, are a true floor. Block floors are considered a floor covering.

▶ **Hardwood Floors**

The term hardwood floors applies to wood floors made of both hardwood and softwood lengths of board.

Among the hardwoods, oak, beech, birch, maple and pecan are the most common. The most common among the softwoods are pine, fir, redwood and hemlock.

The softwoods are usually less expensive than the hardwoods. However, they tend to wear more rapidly and show abrasions more readily than hardwoods.

Hardwood floors include both strip and plank flooring. Strip flooring ranges in width from 1-1/2 to 3-1/4 inches. Plank flooring is available in widths of 3 to 9 inches. Both are available in thicknesses of 3/8 to 3/4 inches.

Two types of milled edges are available for both strip and plank boards:

- Tongue and groove edges
- Square edges

Tongue and groove boards have a tongue on one edge and one end of the board, while the other edge and end have grooves. During installation, the tongue portions of one board must interlock with the groove portions of adjacent boards. Generally, strip flooring is available only with tongue and groove, while plank flooring may or may not be milled in that manner.

Hardwood Floors

Square edged boards are cut squarely at each edge and end. During installation, each board is butted tightly against other boards to form the joint.

Both strip and plank flooring are installed with nails. Tongue and groove boards are blind nailed, while square edge boards are face nailed.

For plank flooring, you may want to install pegs at the end of each board. Wooden pegs were once used to install planks. Pegs can be used to achieve an original effect.

Planks are nailed in the normal manner, then holes drilled and filled with the pegs. It is customary to use pegs of a different wood than the plank for a contrasting appearance.

▶ **Block Floors**

Block floors are commonly available in oak, maple, birch, beech, pecan and hemlock. Blocks may be constructed in several different ways:

- A solid one-piece construction
- Small sections of wood joined together
- Laminated layers of wood

Because of the different methods of construction, blocks are available with patterns and unique designs made by forming each block from different grains, textures and directions.

The most common block floors are available in squares and rectangles ranging in width and length from 4 to 12 inches. Thicknesses vary from 1/4 to 3/4 inches.

Two types of milled edges are available for wood blocks:

- Tongue and groove edges
- Square edges

Tongue and groove blocks have a tongue on two edges and a groove on the opposite two edges. During installation, the tongue edges must interlock with the groove edges of adjacent blocks.

Square edged blocks are cut squarely at each edge. During installation, each block is butted tightly against each other block to form the joint.

Block floors are commonly installed with adhesive. No nailing is required.

▶ **Planning and Estimating**

Install a hardwood floor in the following sequence:

- Determine type and size of hardwood boards. This is entirely your own preference.
- Remove shoe molding and baseboards.
- Plan the job and estimate the amount of materials needed. See below.
- Obtain any needed tools and supplies. Page 85.
- Check the floor surface. Page 86.
- Install screeds (concrete floors only). Page 86.
- Store and condition boards. Page 85.
- Lay boards. Page 90.
- Refinish floor, if needed. Page 100.
- Install baseboards or molding. Page 100.

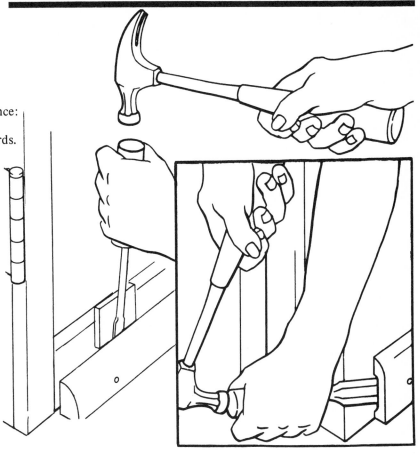

Planning and Estimating

Planning is an important first step in installing hardwood floors. Several areas should be considered before purchasing materials and beginning your installation.

Boards are generally sold in bundles of varying lengths. Because hardwood floors are usually installed parallel to the longest wall, joints [1] between boards in each row will be visible. If you want the fewest number of visible joints, purchase the longest boards for your room.

The pattern of the floor can be varied if you use boards of different widths. For example, installing 4-, 5-, and 9-inch planks [2] can produce a unique personal design. Just be sure to purchase them all in the same thickness. Draw a pattern to use as a guide during installation.

Boards can be purchased either finished or unfinished. Unfinished boards require finishing after they are installed.

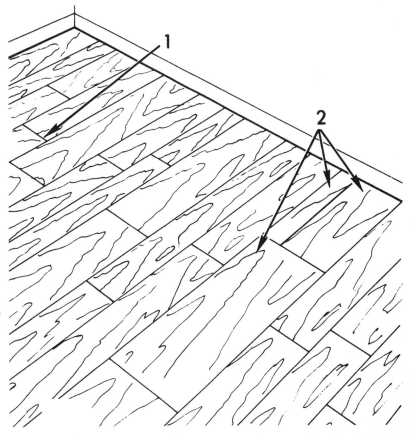

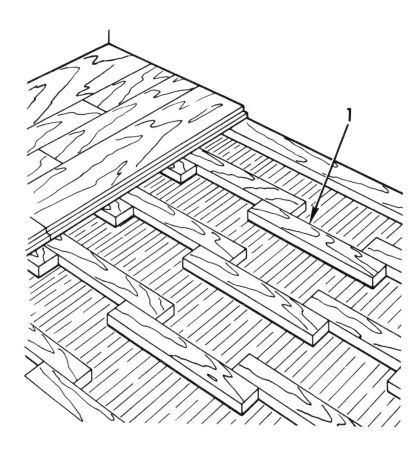

Planning and Estimating

When installing a hardwood floor over concrete, the concrete must be sealed adequately against moisture. Wood screeds [1] are also required to provide a nailing surface for the boards. Be sure the concrete floor is sealed and screeds installed as described on Page 86.

Nails are used to install hardwood floors. The most common nails used to install boards are casing nails and cut flooring nails. Length of nails depends on the thickness of the boards.

Casing nails are used to face nail boards. Cut flooring nails are used to blind nail tongue and groove boards.

Planning and Estimating

To estimate the amount of materials needed you should make a detailed sketch of the floor to be covered. Graph paper is very handy for making this sketch.

Measure and record all dimensions on the sketch.

Take the sketch to a flooring dealer, He will help you determine the following:

● Amount of flooring needed

● Number and type of nails needed

After you purchase the needed materials, boards must be stored in the room in which they are to be installed. They must be allowed to adjust to room temperature and moisture before installation. Be sure to follow instructions for storing and conditioning on Page 86.

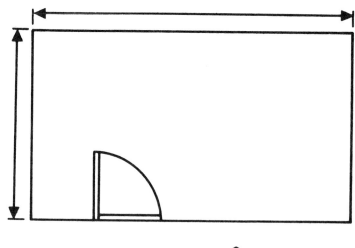

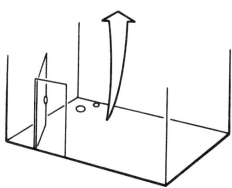

▶ Tools and Supplies

The following tools and supplies are required to install a hardwood floor:

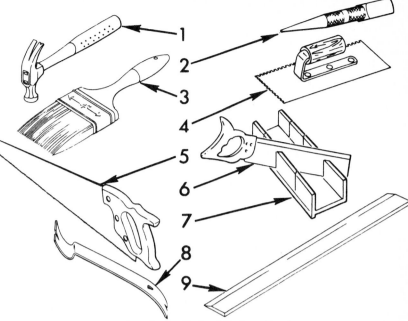

- Hammer [1] and nail set [2] for driving and countersinking nails

- Paintbrush [3] for applying sealer to concrete floors. A paintbrush or notched trowel [4] may be required for applying adhesive to concrete floors.

- Ripsaw [5] for cutting boards with the grain

- Backsaw [6] and miter box [7] for cutting boards against the grain

- Pry bar [8] for forcing boards tightly together during installation

- Ruler [9] for adjusting first row of boards

- String for aligning first row of boards

- Sealer for moistureproofing concrete floors

- Plastic moisture barrier for moisture-proofing extremely damp concrete floors

- 1-1/2 inch casing nails for installing 1 x 4-inch screeds (when installing plastic moisture barrier only)

- Casing nails for face nailing boards. Size depends on board thickness.

- Cut flooring nails for blind nailing tongue and groove boards. Size depends on board thickness.

- Boards

- Wood putty for filling nail holes (face nailing only). Be sure color of putty matches color of boards.

▶ Storing and Conditioning

Hardwood boards are affected by moisture and temperature. For this reason, they must be allowed to adjust to the climate of the room in which they are to be installed.

Never store boards in a damp room, such as a recently plastered room. If installing boards on a concrete floor, moistureproof the floor and install screeds before bringing in the boards.

After the floor is moistureproofed, or the room is as dry as atmospheric conditions permit, do the following:

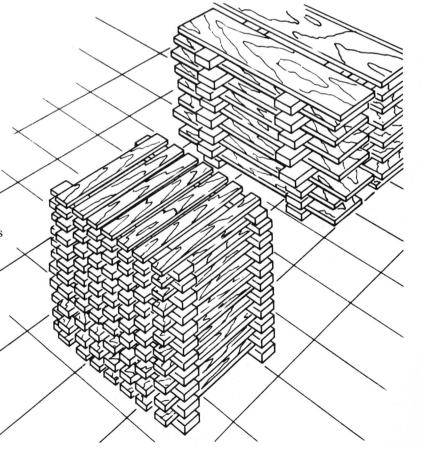

1. Store the boards for at least five days in the room in which they are to be installed. Boards should be loosely stacked to allow air to circulate freely around each piece of wood.

2. Before beginning installation, be sure the room temperature is at least 70°F.

INSTALLING HARDWOOD FLOORS

▶ **Checking Floor Surfaces**

Hardwood floors can be installed on two surfaces:
- Wood subfloor
- Concrete

If you want to lay a hardwood floor over any other surface, remove the old floor covering and check the subsurface.

▶ **Checking a Wood Subfloor**

A hardwood floor cannot be installed over an existing hardwood floor. The subfloor should be plywood sheets installed on joists.

The plywood subfloor must be firm, even and clean before the hardwood boards can be installed.

1. Check that floor is firm and does not move or flex.

If floor is not firm, it must be made firm.

2. Check floor for the following problems:
   - Nails protruding from floor
   - High or low spots
   - Cracks or gaps

If any problems are found, they must be repaired.

3. Thoroughly clean entire floor surface.

▶ **Checking a Concrete Floor**

Installing hardwood floors on concrete requires that wood screeds first be laid to provide a nailing surface. A concrete floor must be level and moistureproofed before the screeds can be installed.

1. Check floor for the following problems:
   - High or low spots
   - Cracks or gaps
   - Moisture

If any problems are found, they must be repaired. A concrete floor can be moistureproofed in two ways. Read Installing Screeds, below, to determine method to be used.

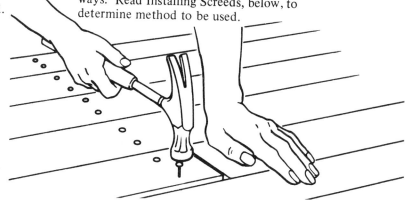

▶ **Installing Screeds**

Screeds are required as a nailing surface to install hardwood floors over a concrete subfloor. Two methods are available for installing screeds. The method used depends upon the dampness of the subfloor.

For slightly damp concrete floors [3], a sealer is first applied to the floor. A moistureproof adhesive [2] is then applied over the sealer. The 2 x 4-inch screeds [1] are placed on the adhesive.

For extremely damp floors [8] a sealer, a moistureproof adhesive [7], a plastic moisture barrier [5], and 1 x 4-inch screeds [4, 6] are needed.

The sealer is applied to the floor [8]. Then the moistureproof adhesive [7] is applied and 1 x 4-inch screeds [6] are placed on the adhesive.

A layer of plastic moisture barrier [5] is then laid over the screeds [6] and a second set of screeds [4] is installed on the first set of screeds.

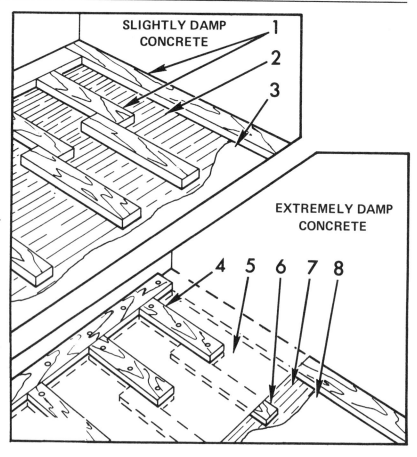

SLIGHTLY DAMP CONCRETE

EXTREMELY DAMP CONCRETE

Installing Screeds

Follow manufacturer's instructions for applying sealer to the floor.

1. Following manufacturer's instructions, apply an even coat of sealer to floor.

Allow sealer to dry according to manufacturer's instructions.

Follow manufacturer's instructions for applying adhesive [1] over the sealer. Some adhesives are applied with a paintbrush while some are applied with a notched trowel.

2. Using paintbrush or notched trowel, apply adhesive [1].

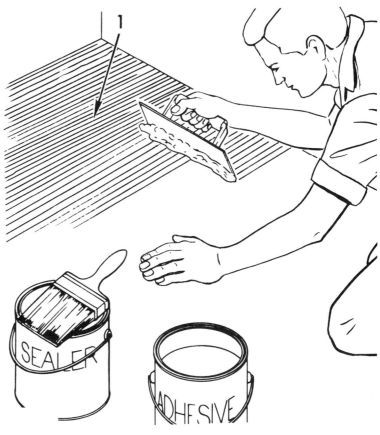

Installing Screeds

Screeds [1] are installed along the entire border of the floor. Screeds [2] must also be installed in rows along the floor with 10-inch intervals between each row. Rows must be installed perpendicular to the direction in which boards are to be installed.

Each row of screeds [2] is made of 18- to 24-inch lengths of wood. Each screed laps the next screed by 4 to 6 inches as shown.

If installing screeds [1, 2] on a slightly damp floor and no plastic moisture barrier is required, screeds are lengths of 2 x 4-inch wood.

If installing screeds [1, 2] on a damp floor and a plastic moisture barrier is required, screeds are lengths of 1 x 4-inch wood.

3. Install necessary screeds [1, 2]. Press each screed firmly into adhesive.

If no plastic moisture barrier is required, go to Page 90 to lay boards.

If plastic moisture barrier is required, go to Page 88.

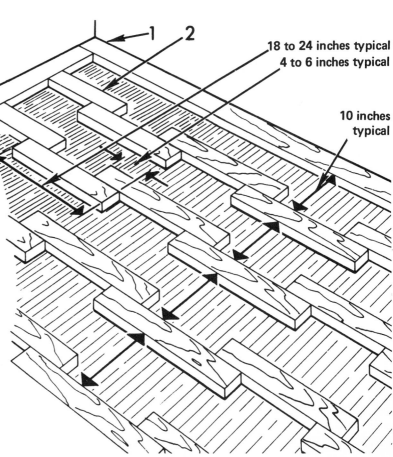

18 to 24 inches typical
4 to 6 inches typical

10 inches typical

INSTALLING HARDWOOD FLOORS

Installing Screeds

Plastic moisture barrier [1] must be laid over the
installed screeds [4]. Do not stretch plastic. Lay
it loosely over installed screeds.

Where two sections of moisture barrier [1] meet,
they must overlap by 3 inches as shown.

4. Install moisture barrier [1] over installed
    screeds [4].

A second set of screeds [3] must now be installed
over the first set of screeds [4]. Be sure that
screeds are the same length as the installed screeds.

Use 1-1/2 inch casing nails [2] to install screeds.
Drive nails flush with surface of screeds.

Nails [2] should be centered on the screed [3]
1/2-inch from the ends. Remaining nails should
be installed at 6-inch intervals along each screed.

5. Install second set of screeds [3].

6. Go to Page 90 to lay boards.

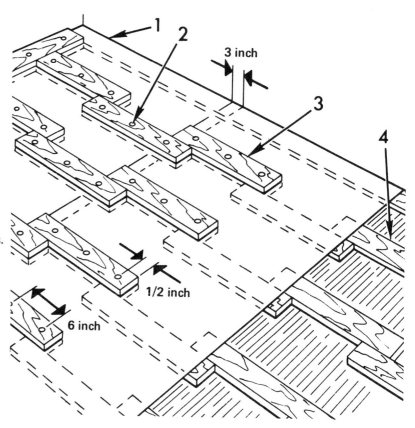

▶ Nailing Methods and Patterns

Two methods of installing nails must be used to
install hardwood floors:

*   Face nailing
*   Blind nailing tongue and groove boards

Face nailing is driving a nail straight down through
the top of the board. Nails are then countersunk
and the holes filled with wood putty.

When face nailing a board, drive the nail to within
approximately 1/4- to 1/8-inch of the surface.

Do not use the hammer to drive the nail flush
with the surface. The hammer head may damage
the flooring. Use a nail set to sink the nail
approximately 1/8-inch below the surface.

Blind nailing is driving a nail at approximately a
50 degree angle into the tongue of a board. Nails
are then countersunk. These holes do not require
filling with wood putty.

When blind nailing, drive the nails to within
approximately 1/4- to 1/8-inch of the tongue
surface. Then use a nail set to sink the nail
approximately 1/8-inch below the surface.

Do not use the hammer to drive the nail flush
with the tongue. The hammer head may damage
the tongue and prevent the next board from
fitting tightly.

The nailing pattern for boards depends upon the
following:

*   Width of board
*   Surface they are being installed on
*   Location of the board

Tongue and groove boards need to be face nailed
along the first and last rows. All remaining boards
are blind nailed.

Tongue and groove plank flooring, because of its
width, may require both blind nailing and face
nailing for each board.

Square edged boards require face nailing only.

Nailing Methods and Patterns

Nails are installed as shown for the following boards:

A   First row installed on screeds
B   Middle rows installed on screeds
C   Last two rows installed on screeds

D   First row installed on wood subfloor
E   Middle rows installed on wood subfloor
F   Last two rows installed on wood subfloor

Note that for strip tongue and groove boards, the first and last row must be face nailed. The next to last row is not nailed at all.

For square edged boards, nails are installed at the same intervals as shown. Instead of blind nailing at the tongue, two nails [1] are face nailed at each interval.

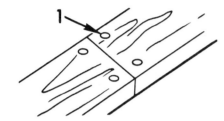

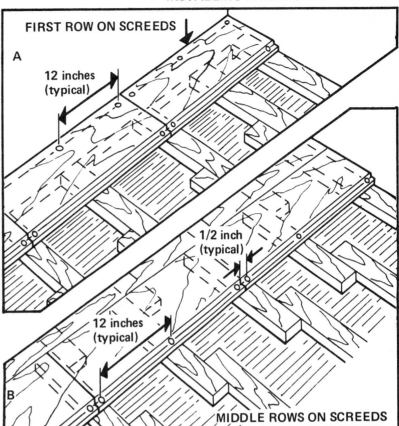

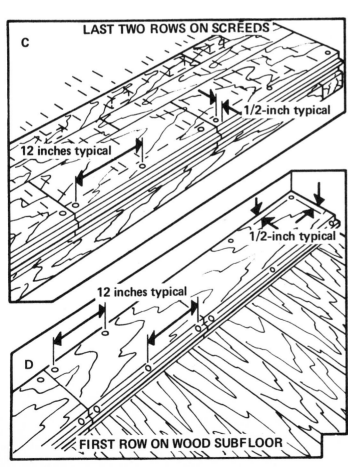

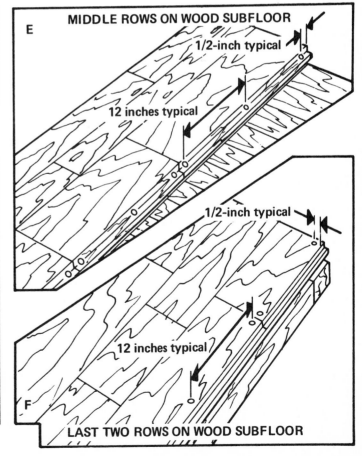

INSTALLING HARDWOOD FLOORS

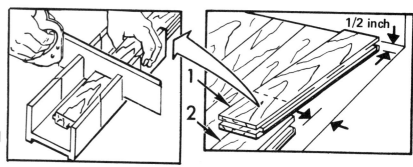

▶ **Cutting Boards**

Cutting boards may be required in the following situations:

- First and last boards [1, 3] in each row
- To fill the gap [6] between the last row [4] and wall

First and last boards [1,3] in a row must fit tightly against middle boards [2]. Leave a 1/2-inch gap [6] at the walls to allow for expansion of the floor and walls.

For first boards [1] in a row, be sure groove end is cut off. For last boards [3], be sure tongue end is cut off. To measure, board [1, 3] is positioned 1/2-inch from wall and over board [2]. A mark is placed at the location of the cut and the board is cut with a backsaw and miter box.

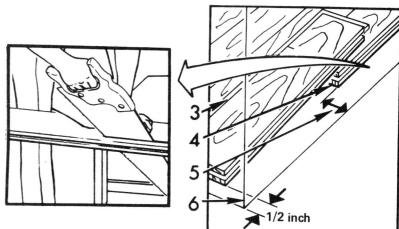

Between the last row [4] and wall, measure gap [5]. Boards to fill the gap must be cut with a ripsaw along their entire length. Be sure to cut off tongue edge of boards.

▶ **Laying Boards**

These procedures describe the installation of tongue and groove boards. Square edge boards are installed the same way, except that they are face nailed instead of blind nailed. Otherwise, the procedures are applicable.

Before laying the boards, read the following sections:

- Storing and Conditioning, Page 85.
- Checking Floor Surfaces, Page 86.
- Nailing Methods and Patterns, Page 88.
- Cutting Boards, above.

Because walls are seldom perfectly straight, the boards should not be aligned with the wall. Instead, a piece of string should be stretched alongside the wall, and the boards aligned to the string.

1. Make a mark 12 inches from the wall. Make another mark 12 inches from the other end of the wall.

2. Drive a tack part way into each mark. Tie a string [2] tightly between the tacks [1].

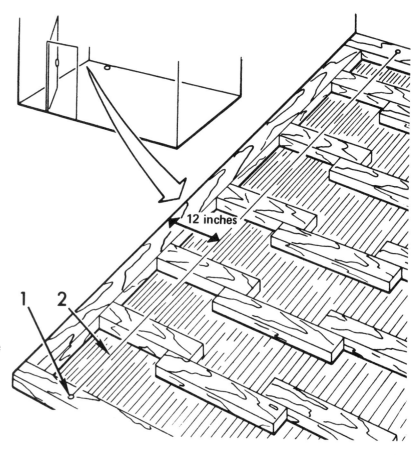

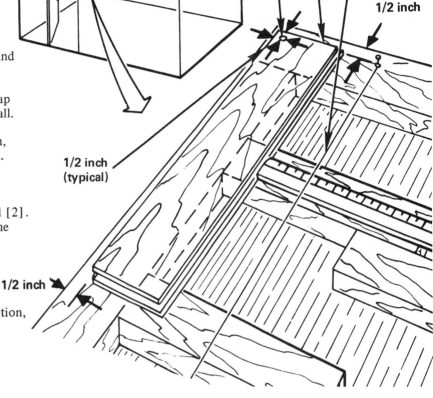

1/2 inch

1/2 inch
(typical)

1/2 inch

Laying Boards

First board [2] is installed with groove end and groove edge facing the walls.

3. Place board [2] at wall with 1/2-inch gap between board and side wall and end wall.

4. While holding board [2] at this position, face nail one nail [1] at distance shown.

Board will now pivot on installed nail [1].

String [3] and a ruler are used to align board [2]. The tongue edge must be equidistant from the string for its entire length.

5. Using ruler, align board [2] with string [3].

6. While holding board [2] at aligned position, install necessary nails.

Laying Boards

The next board [1] is installed by inserting its groove end over the tongue end of the preceding board [3]. If board [1] is the last board in the row, be sure to leave a 1/2-inch gap between the end of the board and the wall.

7. Place next board [1] at installed position. Using ruler, align board with string [2].

8. While holding board [1] at aligned position, install necessary nails.

Repeat Steps 7 and 8 for the remaining boards in the first row except for the last board in the row. The last board may have to be measured and cut before installing. Then repeat Steps 7 and 8 to install the last board.

The next four rows of boards [6] should be cut and arranged on the floor before nailing to be sure they are in the correct position. Be sure to leave a 1/2-inch gap between the ends of the rows [6] and the walls.

Joints [4] at ends of boards in adjacent rows [5] must be staggered. Be sure that distance between joints [4] in adjacent rows [5] is at least 6 inches.

If installing boards on screeds, make joints in adjacent rows on different screeds. This may require that the boards be cut to different lengths.

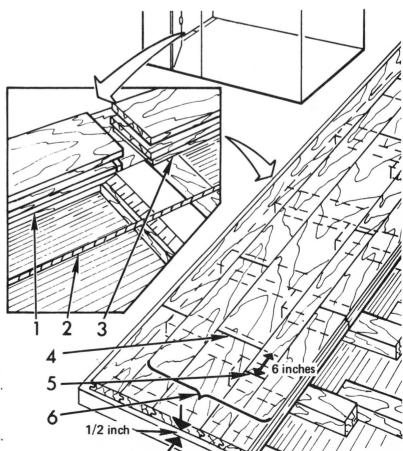

1/2 inch

6 inches

INSTALLING HARDWOOD FLOORS

Laying Boards

9.   Cut and arrange next four rows [1].

After the four rows [1] are cut and arranged, each row must be nailed to the floor. Install each row in its entirety before installing next row.

Each board [3] is installed by placing its groove edge over the tongue edge of adjacent row [2].

10.   Place board [3] at installed position. Press board tightly against installed row [2].

11.   While holding board [3] at installed position, install necessary nails.

12.   Repeat Steps 10 and 11 to install all boards in four rows [1].

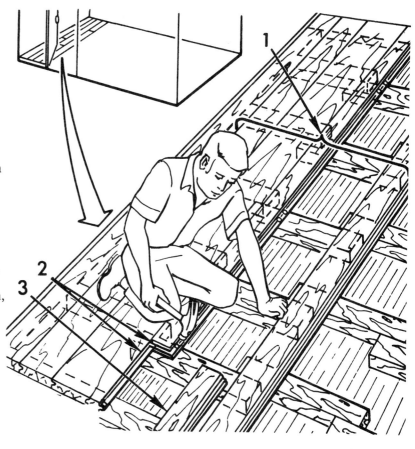

Laying Boards

After every four rows [1] are installed, boards must be forced tightly against each other.

Begin at one end of last row installed and work to the other end.

13.   Place scrap board [3] against installed board [2]. Using hammer, strike scrap board sharply. Repeat along entire length of row.

Repeat Steps 9 through 13 until all but last two rows are installed.

The last two rows [4] must be cut and arranged before nailing. Be sure to leave a 1/2-inch gap between first and last boards in a row and the walls.

14.   Cut and arrange last two rows [4].

For tongue and groove boards, last two rows [4] cannot be blind nailed because there is not enough room to use a hammer without damaging the wall. Because of this, next to last row [5] is not nailed at all and the last row [6] is face nailed.

For square edged boards, the last two rows [4] are face nailed in the same way as preceding rows.

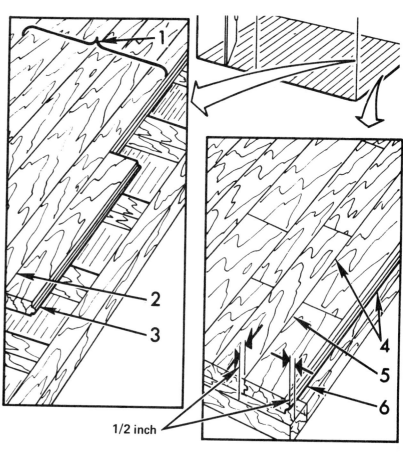

1/2 inch

Laying Boards

A pry bar is used to force the last two rows [1] tightly against installed boards [5]. A piece of cardboard should be used to protect the wall.

Begin at one corner and work to the other corner, nailing one board at a time.

15.   Using pry bar, force board [3] tightly against installed board [5]. Install necessary nails.

Repeat Step 15 until all boards in last row are nailed.

If gap [2] between last row and wall is too large to be covered by baseboards or molding, lengths of boards must be cut to fit. Boards are then installed using instructions in Step 15.

Wood putty to fill holes[4] where nails have been countersunk must be the same color as the boards.

16.   Using wood putty, fill all nail holes [4].

If boards are pre-finished with no finihshing required, go to Page 100 to install baseboards or molding.

If finishing is required, go to Page 100.

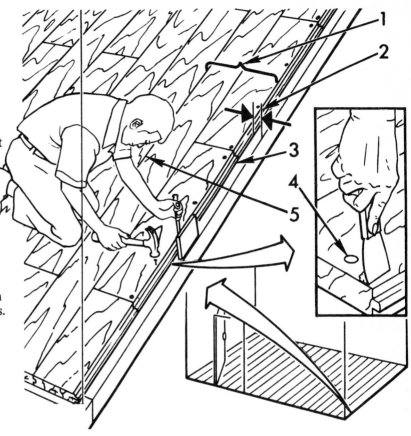

═══ INSTALLING BLOCK FLOORS ═══

▶ **Planning and Estimating**

Install a block floor in the following sequence:

- Determine the type and size of blocks. This is entirely your own preference.
- Remove shoe molding or baseboards.
- Estimate the amount of materials needed. Page 94.
- Obtain any needed tools and supplies. Page 94.
- Check the floor surface. Page 95.
- Store and condition blocks. Page 95.
- Square off the floor. Page 96.
- Lay blocks. Page 98.
- Install baseboards or molding. Page 100.

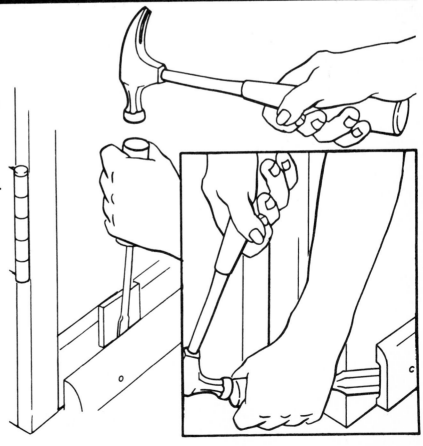

INSTALLING BLOCK FLOORS

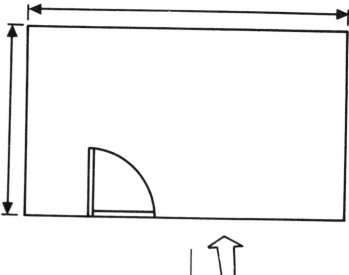

Planning and Estimating

To estimate the amount of materials needed
you should make a detailed sketch of the floor to
be covered. Graph paper is very handy for making
this sketch.

Measure and record all dimensions on the sketch.

Take the sketch to a flooring dealer. He will help
you determine the following:

● Number of blocks needed

● Type and amount of adhesive needed

After you purchase needed materials, wood
blocks must be stored in the room in which they
are to be installed. They must be allowed to adjust
to room temperature and moisture before installation. Be sure to follow instructions for storing
and conditioning on Page 95.

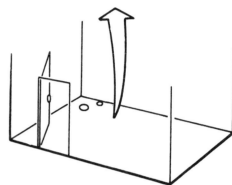

▶ **Tools and Supplies**

The following tools and supplies are required to
install a block floor:

● Chalk line [1] for squaring off the floor

● Crosscut saw [2] for cutting straight edges
in blocks

● Coping saw [3] for cutting around
obstructions

● Paintbrush [4] or notched trowel [5] for
applying adhesive

● Cloths for removing excess adhesive from
face of blocks

● Adhesive

● Blocks

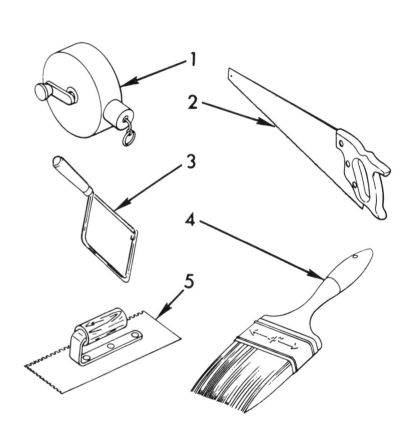

▶ **Storing and Conditioning**

Wood blocks are affected by moisture and temperature. For this reason, they must be allowed to adjust to the climate of the room in which they are to be installed.

Never store blocks in a damp room, such as a recently plastered room. If installing blocks on a concrete floor, moistureproof the floor before bringing in the blocks.

After the floor is moistureproofed, or the room is as dry as atmospheric conditions permit, do the following.

1. Store the blocks for at least five days in the room in which they are to be installed. Blocks should be loosely stacked to allow air to circulate freely around each piece of wood.

2. Before beginning installation, be sure the room temperature is at least 70°F.

Checking Floor Surfaces

Block flooring can be installed on the following surfaces:

- Wood
- Concrete
- Resilient

Because block floors are rigid, they cannot take the shape of the subfloor. For this reason, the floor must be flat and smooth.

The subfloor must be rigid because a subfloor which flexes under the block flooring may cause the blocks to crack, or gaps to form at the seams.

▶ **Checking a Wood Floor**

A wood floor must be firm, even and clean before a block floor can be installed.

It is not recommended that a block floor be laid directly over a hardwood floor. An underlayment grade of plywood, particle board or hardboard should be installed.

1. Check that floor is firm and does not move or flex.

If floor is not firm, it must be made firm.

2. Check floor for following problems:

- Protruding nails
- Loose boards
- High or low spots
- Cracks or gaps

If problems are found, they must be repaired.

3. Clean entire floor surface.

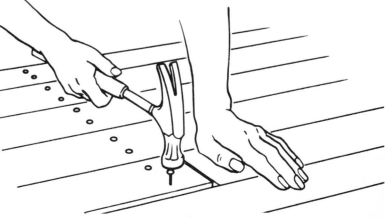

INSTALLING BLOCK FLOORS

▶ **Checking a Concrete Floor**

A concrete floor must be level, clean and moistureproofed before block flooring can be installed.

1. Check floor for the following problems:

    - High or low spots
    - Cracks or gaps
    - Moisture

If any problems are found, they must be repaired.

2. Clean floor surface to remove all oil, dirt and grease.

Because wood blocks are affected by moisture, the floor must be moistureproofed.

For dry or slightly moist concrete, a sealer is all that is needed. For moist concrete, a sealer and plastic moisture barrier is needed. Check with your dealer about the type of moistureproofing you should use.

3. Moistureproof floor. Refer to Page 88 for a description of plastic moisture barrier.

▶ **Checking a Resilient Floor**

A resilient floor must be even, securely installed and clean before block flooring can be installed.

If old resilient floor is badly damaged, it should be removed completely. If damaged resilient tiles or sheets become loose, it could cause damage to the block floor.

If removing old floor covering, be sure to remove or smooth old adhesive before installing new floor.

1. Check floor for the following problems:

    - Loose tiles, sheets or pieces
    - Cracks or holes

If any problems are found, they must be repaired.

A commercial wax remover should be used to remove old wax.

2. Remove all old wax from floor.

▶ **Squaring Off the Floor**

Chalk lines [2,4] must be marked to provide a guide for laying blocks squarely on the floor.

1. Locate the centers of two opposite walls. Place marks [1,3] on the floor at each center.

2. Attach chalk line to mark [1]. Pull chalk line to mark [3].

3. While holding chalk line tight between marks [1,3], pull line straight up from floor and release.

Chalk line will mark a straight line [2] on the floor.

4. Repeat Steps 1 through 3 to mark a line [4] between other two opposite walls.

Narrow blocks along the borders of the floor are less attractive than wider blocks. The chalk lines may have to be relocated to provide proper borders. Go to Page 97 to check and adjust borders.

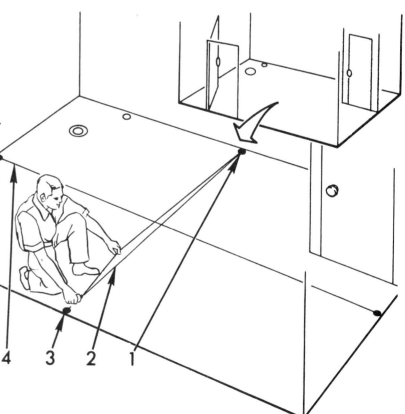

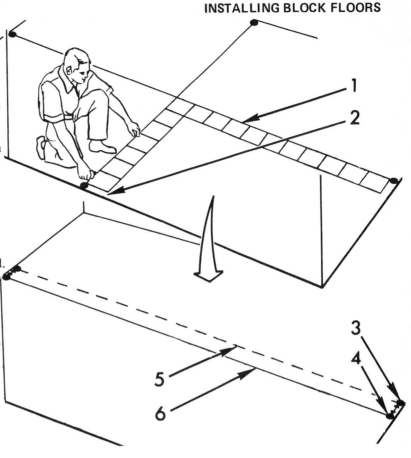

Squaring Off the Floor

5. Beginning where chalk lines cross, lay blocks in two rows [1] as shown.

6. For each row, measure distance [2] between wall and last whole block.

If distance between block and wall is greater than 1/2 width of a block, chalk line is correctly located. Go to Page 98 to lay blocks.

If distance between block and wall is less than 1/2 width of a block, chalk line must be relocated. Continue.

7. Make new marks [3] 1/2 width of a block away from old marks [4]. Locate marks [3] in direction away from wall with narrow border.

8. Make a new chalk line [5] parallel to old chalk line [6].

▶ **Measuring and Cutting Border Tiles**

After all whole blocks in a section have been laid, measure and cut the blocks for the borders. Each border block is measured and cut individually.

The following procedures show how to measure and mark a border block quickly and accurately.

1. Place a loose block [2] on top of the last whole block [1] in any row. Align edges of blocks [1,2].

If tongue and groove blocks are being installed, be sure that edges of blocks [1,2] will mate after cutting.

2. Place another block [3] on top of block [2]. Edge of block [3] must be parallel to wall and 1/8-inch from wall.

3. Using edge of block [3] as a guide, make a mark [4] on block [2].

4. Using crosscut saw, cut block along mark.

Piece [5] of block [2] is installed in border.

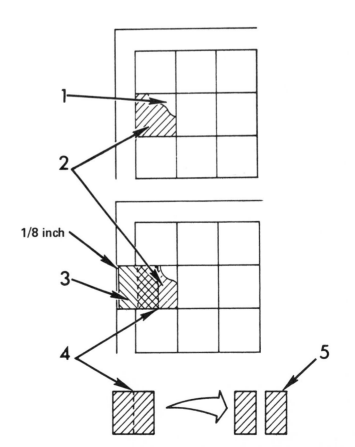

97

INSTALLING BLOCK FLOORS

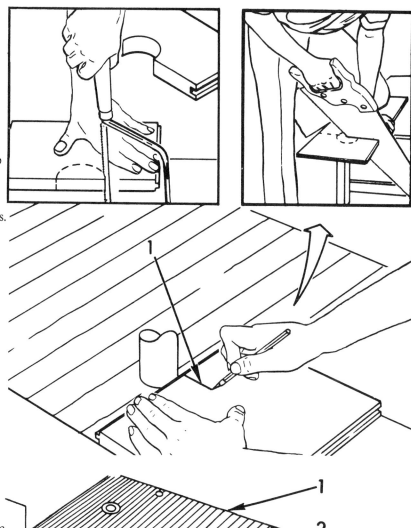

Measuring and Cutting around Obstructions

Measuring and cutting around obstructions generally requires making a paper pattern of the desired shape. The pattern is then transferred to the top side of the block for cutting.

Whole blocks [1] may require cutting into two sections to fit around posts or other obstructions.

When tracing the pattern on the block [1], plan your cut so that any grain patterns match. If installing tongue and groove blocks, be sure mating edges are correct.

A crosscut saw is used to make straight cuts. However, a coping saw is used for curved and irregular cuts.

▶ Laying Blocks

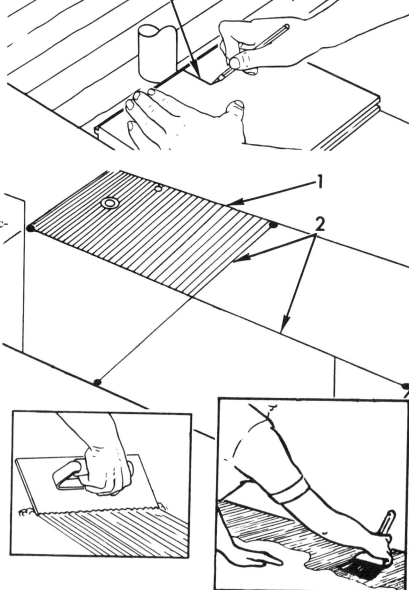

Before laying blocks, be sure to allow them to adjust to the climate of the room. Follow instructions for storing and conditioning on Page 95.

Floor must be squared off. Page 96.

Read through this entire procedure before beginning to lay blocks.

Blocks are laid in one section of the floor at a time. Both whole blocks and blocks around the border are laid before going to the next section.

Begin in a section [1] away from the entryway. Plan to finish at the entryway.

Adhesive may be applied with either a notched trowel or a paintbrush. Be sure to follow manufacturer's instructions for proper method of application.

When applying adhesive, be careful not to cover chalk lines [2].

1. Apply an even coat of adhesive to entire section [1]. Allow adhesive to set up according to manufacturer's instructions.

Laying Blocks

First block [2] is laid where chalk lines [1, 3] cross. Remaining blocks are laid in sequence as shown. Butt each block tightly against adjacent block.

You may have to stand or kneel on laid blocks to complete a section. Be careful not to move them out of position.

Some manufacturers specify the direction that the grain of each block must run. Many times the direction of the grain is alternated with each block as shown.[4]. By changing grain direction, the effects of expansion are minimized.

When laying tongue and groove blocks [5], align the tongue and groove and lower the block into position.

For all blocks, lay them into position. Do not slide them. Sliding the blocks removes the adhesive from the floor and may force some adhesive onto the surface of the blocks. Have a damp cloth handy to wipe off excess adhesive before it dries.

Laying Blocks

All whole blocks [3] are laid first. If an obstruction [1] is in the center of the section, blocks must be cut to fit as they are being laid. Page 98 describes measuring and cutting around obstructions.

2. Following sequence as shown, lay all whole blocks [3]. Press each block firmly over its entire surface as it is laid.

Blocks [2] along borders of the section must be cut to fit one at a time. Page 97 describes measuring and cutting blocks at borders of the floor.

3. Cut and lay blocks [2] along borders of section.

4. Repeat Pages 98 through 99 to lay blocks in remaining sections.

After entire floor is laid, baseboards or molding must be installed. Page 100.

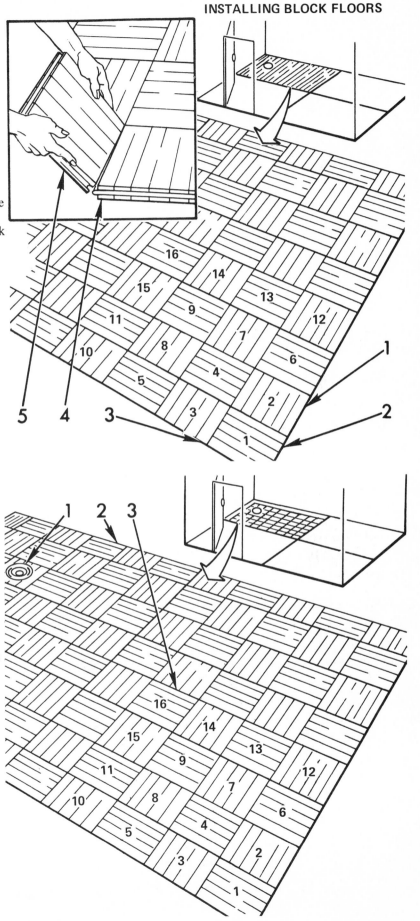

INSTALLING BASEBOARDS OR MOLDING

Either wood or vinyl baseboards and molding may be used with wood floors. Wood baseboards are by far the most common.

If you plan to install vinyl cove molding [1], see Page 34 for installation procedures.

If you plan to install wood baseboards or molding, one of the following applications may apply to your situation.

● Install baseboard only. This application is the most common. It should be used if gap [2] between floor and wall is narrow enough to be covered by baseboard.

● Install baseboard and shoe molding. If gap [3] between floor and wall is too wide to be covered by baseboard alone, install shoe molding also.

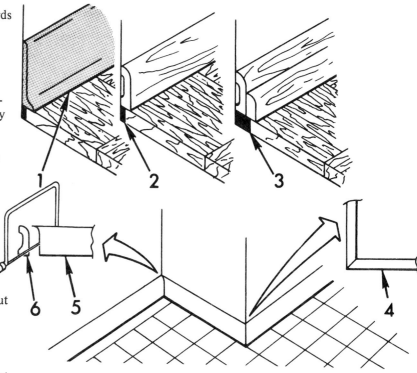

For both shoe molding and baseboards, make cut for joints as follows:

● Outside corners – use 45 degree miter cut [4]

● Inside corners – use coping cut. Coping cut is made by cutting board [5] to fit closely against board [6].

REFINISHING HARDWOOD FLOORS

▶ **Refinishing**

Old floors which show their wear may be made to look new again by refinishing. Even newly installed hardwood floors, if unfinished, must be finished.

The following tools and supplies are required to refinish a hardwood floor:

● Drum sander [1] is used to remove old finish and smooth the bare wood. It can be rented from flooring dealers or tool rental companies. When renting a drum sander, be sure to ask for operating instructions and for instructions on changing abrasive paper.

● Floor edger [2] is used for removing old finish and smoothing the bare wood at floor edges. It can be rented from a flooring dealer or tool rental company. When renting an edger, be sure to ask for operating instructions and for instructions on changing abrasive paper.

● Sanding block [3] for removing old finish and smoothing the bare wood at areas inacessible to drum sander or floor edger.

● Hammer [4] and nail set [5]

● Putty knife [6]
● Vacuum cleaner
● Tack mop
● Wood putty
● Wax remover—be sure to get wax remover, not cleaning wax.

● Abrasive paper. Use quality abrasive paper.

  For drum sander
  Grade 20, 36, and 80

  For floor edger
  Grade 20 and 60

  For sanding block
  Coarse and Medium

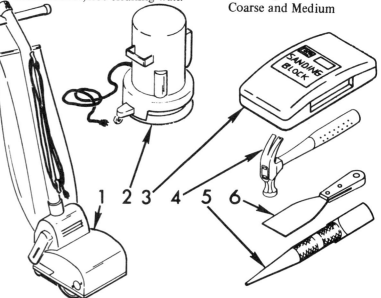

Refinishing

The finish must be selected to apply to the sanded floor. Five basic finishes are available for hardwood floors:

- Penetrating floor seal
- Varnish
- Shellac
- Lacquer
- Polyurethane

Each has its own advantages, but for wearability and lasting beauty polyurethane is probably the best.

Ask a paint dealer about the different types. He will be helpful in selecting the finish you desire.

Before beginning to refinish a floor, all furniture must be removed. Because of the amount of dust generated by the sanding, it is better to remove all drapes, pictures and other wall accessories before beginning.

For the best looking job, shoe molding, if installed, should be removed. You may even wish to remove baseboards to work closer to wall.

▶ **Surface Preparation**

When refinishing existing hardwood floors, all old wax must be removed and the surface prepared before the floor can be sanded. A commercial wax remover is used to remove all old wax from floor.

1. Remove all old wax from floor.
2. Check that there are no loose or squeaking boards [1].

If loose or squeaking boards are found, they must be repaired. Page 107.

3. Check that there are no damaged boards [1].

If damaged boards are found, they must be replaced. Page 104.

4. Check that there are no splinters [2].

If splinters are found, glue splinters to floor with wood glue.

5. Check that all nailheads [3] are driven below floor surface.

If nailheads are found above floor surface, drive them below the surface with a hammer and nail set. Then fill with wood putty.

6. Go to Page 102 to sand the floor.

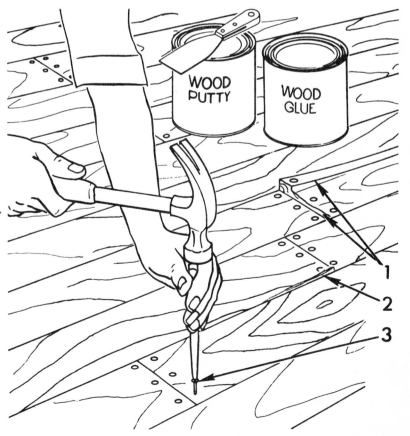

REFINISHING HARDWOOD FLOORS

▶ **Using a Drum Sander**

Regardless of what grade of abrasive paper is used, a drum sander [1] is used the same way for each grade.

When renting a drum sander, be sure to ask for instructions on installing abrasive paper.

CAUTION

Be sure that the sanding drum [2] is not touching floor when sander is turned on. The sander will start rapidly across the floor and could make gouges or grooves in the floor.

Before lowering sanding drum [2], be sure you have a firm grip on sander, and you are moving the sander forward.

Always move the sander in the direction of the wood grain, which is parallel to the length of the wood boards.

Be sure to clean the dust bag [3] at regular intervals.

Begin at one wall and sand in one strip to opposite wall. Then turn and sand the next strip to the beginning wall.

Overlap each strip by at least 3 inches.

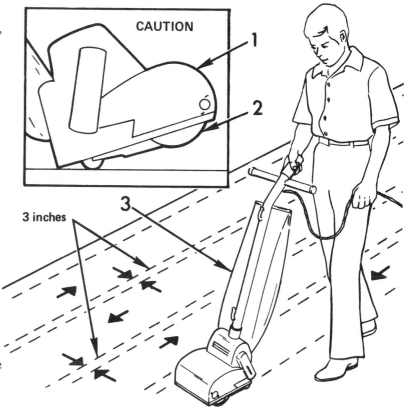

▶ **Sanding the Floor**

If refinishing an existing hardwood floor, surface must be prepared. Page 101.

Before sanding the floor, be sure to read Using a Drum Sander, above.

If refinishing a newly laid floor, go to Page 103.

An existing hardwood floor must be sanded to remove all the old finish and to expose smooth, bare wood.

Sanding is accomplished by using different grades of sandpaper. Start with coarser paper first and work to fine paper.

Grade 20 abrasive paper is used with the drum sander and floor edger to remove most of the old finish.

1. Using drum sander, sand all floor that can be reached.

2. Using floor edger [1], sand all floor edges that can be reached.

Inaccessible areas, such as corners, must be sanded with a sanding block and coarse abrasive paper.

3. Using sanding block [2], sand all unsanded areas.

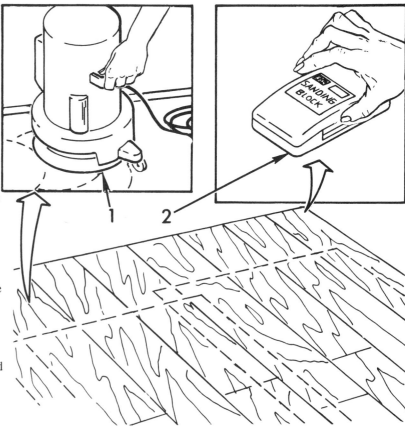

Sanding the Floor

Grade 36 abrasive paper is used with the drum sander to smooth the surface.

4. Using drum sander, sand all floor that can be reached.

Floor must be checked for cracks and gaps.

5. Carefully check that there are no cracks [2] or gaps [1] in floor surface.

If cracks or gaps are found, they must be filled with wood putty. Do not continue until wood putty has dried according to manufacturer's instructions.

Sanding the Floor

Grade 60 abrasive paper is used with the floor edger to make edges of floor smooth.

6. Using floor edger, sand all floor edges that can be reached.

A sanding block and medium abrasive paper is used to smooth areas of the floor inaccessible to drum sander and edger.

7. Using sanding block, sand all unsanded areas.

The next sanding is the final sanding. Because you will be working on a smooth floor, wear soft shoes or no shoes until finish is applied.

Grade 80 abrasive paper is used with drum sander to remove all scratches and leave wood smooth.

8. Using drum sander, sand all floor that can be reached.

9. Go to **Page 104** to apply finish.

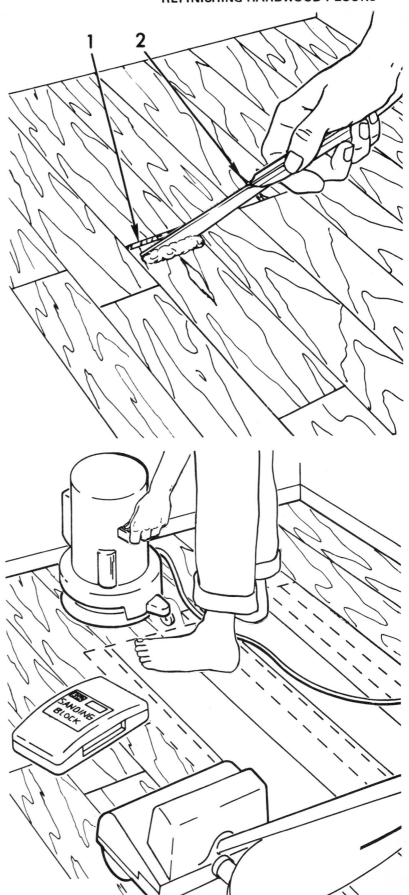

REFINISHING HARDWOOD FLOORS

▶ **Applying the Finish**

Before a finish can be applied, all dust must be removed from the room, and the floor must be absolutely clean.

Be sure to remove dust on windowsills, baseboards and other fixtures in the room.

1. Using vacuum cleaner, dust room and floor.

2. Using tack mop, dust floor.

Finish can now be applied to the floor. Follow manufacturer's instructions for the following requirements:

● Type of applicator
● Drying time
● Number of coats needed

3. Apply finish to floor.

4. After required coats of finish have dried, install baseboards or molding, if necessary. Page 100.

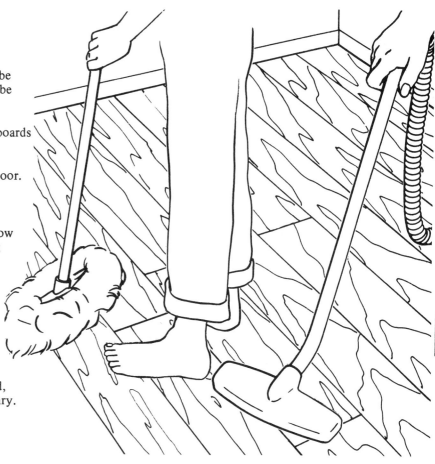

REPAIRING HARDWOOD FLOORS

▶ **Replacing Damaged Boards**

If the boards are installed on screeds or joists, it may be simpler to remove the whole board rather than try to locate the screeds.

The following tools and supplies are required:

> Drill and large wood bit [1]
> Hammer [2]
> Nail set [3]
> Sharp 1-inch wood chisel [4]
> Miter box and backsaw [5]
> Putty knife [6]
> Wood glue
> Block of wood
> Wood putty – same color as replacement board
> Replacement board. Same thickness and type as damaged board.
> Finishing nails
> Medium grit sandpaper

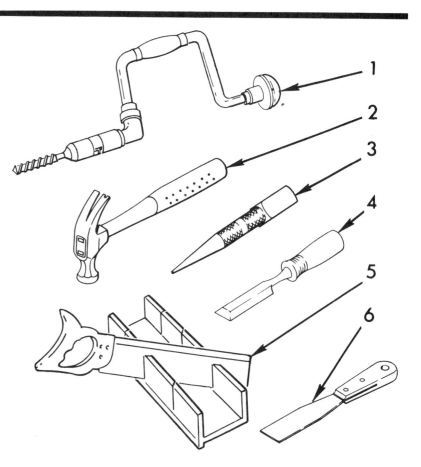

Replacing Damaged Boards

If board is installed on screeds or directly to floor joists, line [1] must be made in center of screed or joists.

1.　Draw a line [1] perpendicular to board at each end of damaged area.

When drilling through board, be careful not to drill deeply into subfloor.

2.　Using large wood bit, drill a series of overlapping holes [2] at each line.

If boards are tongue and groove boards, be careful not to damage tongue and groove of adjacent boards.

3.　Using hammer and 1-inch wood chisel, split damaged board [3] down the center.

When removing the damaged board [3], be sure to remove the tongue of the damaged board from the groove of the adjacent board, if required.

4.　Pry out damaged board [3]. Remove all nails used to secure damaged board.

Replacing Damaged Boards

5.　Using hammer and 1-inch chisel, cut both edges [1] of installed boards square and even.

6.　Place replacement board [3] at opening [2]. Mark board to length of opening.

A miter box and backsaw should be used to insure a square cut at both ends of the board.

7.　Using miter box and backsaw, cut board [3] at marks.

If installing square edge board, go to Step 10. If installing tongue and groove board, continue.

The lower half of the groove [4] must be removed, so that the board can be placed over the tongue of the installed board.

8.　Using hammer and chisel, remove lower half of groove [4].

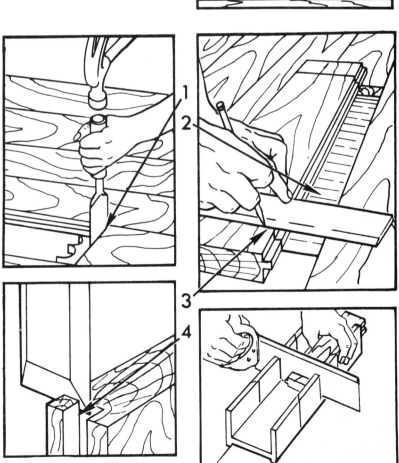

REPAIRING HARDWOOD FLOORS

Replacing Damaged Boa.

Before applying glue, be sure that board fits securely in opening.

A coat of wood glue must be applied to the tongue [4] and groove [3] of replacement board and to the tongue [1] and groove [2] of adjacent boards.

9.   Apply a coat of wood glue to tongues [1, 4] and grooves [2, 3].

To install tongue and groove boards, place tongue [4] of replacement board into groove [2] of adjacent board.

10.   Install board [5] into opening.

11.   Using hammer and block of wood, tap board [5] until level with adjacent boards.

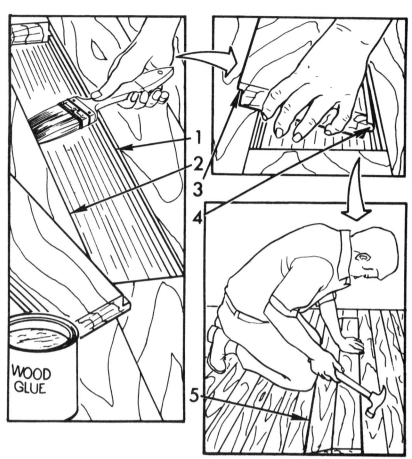

Replacing Damaged Boards

Nails are now installed to hold the board to the floor. Four pilot holes [1], smaller than the nails, should be drilled to prevent nails from splitting the board.

12.   Using small drill bit, drill four pilot holes [1] into board.

When driving nails [2] into the board, drive nails to within 1/4-inch of surface. Then use nail set to countersink nails approximately 1/8-inch below the surface.

13.   Using hammer and nail set, countersink nails [2] into pilot holes [1].

14.   Using putty knife and wood putty, fill all holes [3]. Allow putty to dry. Sand putty level with board.

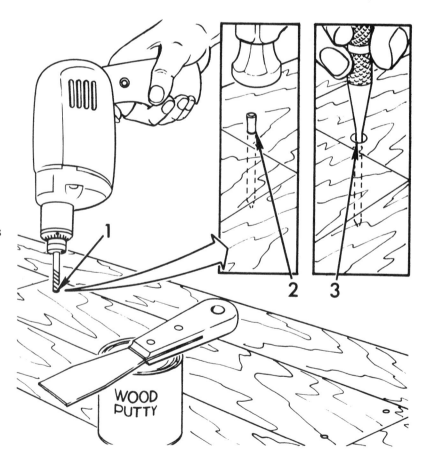

▶ **Repairing Squeaking Boards**

Instructions in this section show how to repair a squeaking board installed on a wood subfloor.

A squeaking floor is usually caused by a loose board rubbing against adjacent boards or nails.

The following tools and supplies are required:

Drill and small bit [1]. Bit should be slightly smaller than diameter of nails.
Hammer [2]
Nail set [3]
Putty knife [4]
Annular ring nails [5] or spiral nails [6]
Wood putty — same color as board

A loose board can usually be located by walking over the board and listening for it to squeak.

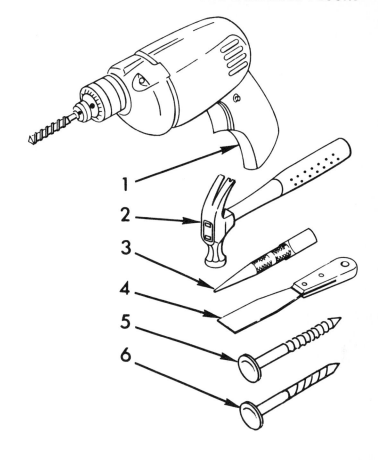

Repairing Squeaking Boards

Pilot holes [3] must be drilled into boards at a 75° angle [1]. Measure length of board [4] and mark center. Begin nailing at center of board [4] and work toward both ends.

1. Using drill and bit, drill two pilot holes [3] in center of board [4].

When driving nails [2] into the board, drive nails to within 1/4-inch of surface. Then use nail set to countersink nails approximately 1/8-inch below the surface.

2. Using hammer and nail set, countersink two nails [2] in two pilot holes [3].

3. Using putty knife and wood putty, fill two holes [3].

Check that board does not squeak or move.

If board squeaks or moves, repeat Steps 1 through 3 at 6-inch intervals along board.

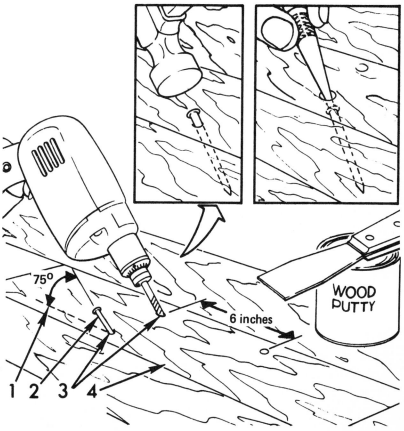